Ethical Decisions
in Physical Education
and Sport

Ethical Decisions in Physical Education and Sport

By

EDWARD J. SHEA

Department of Physical Education
Southern Illinois University
Carbondale, Illinois

CHARLES C THOMAS • PUBLISHER
Springfield • Illinois • U.S.A.

Published and Distributed Throughout the World by

CHARLES C THOMAS ● PUBLISHER

Bannerstone House

301-327 East Lawrence Avenue, Springfield, Illinois, U.S.A.

© *1978, by* CHARLES C THOMAS ● PUBLISHER

ISBN 0-398-03787-6

Library of Congress Catalog Card Number: 77-871

With THOMAS BOOKS *careful attention is given to all details of
manufacturing and design. It is the Publisher's desire to present books that
are satisfactory as to their physical qualities and artistic possibilities and
appropriate for their particular use.* THOMAS BOOKS *will be true to those
laws of quality that assure a good name and good will.*

Printed in the United States of America
OO-2

Library of Congress Cataloging in Publication Data

Shea, Edward J
   Ethical decisions in physical education and
sport.

   Bibliography: p.
   Includes index.
   1. Physical education and training--Moral
and religious aspects. 2. Decision-making
(Ethics) I. Title.
GV14.35.S48   375'.6137   77-871
ISBN 0-398-03787-6

PREFACE

Nature of the Text

THIS text has been written in an effort to encourage teachers of physical education to (1) revise the content of courses on principles of physical education so as to replace repetitious material from other courses with an important component of study in professional preparation, namely, the ethical and moral values of professional actions, and (2) to consider the introduction of a specific course on ethics and morality into the professional curriculum at the undergraduate and/or graduate levels of study.

The aim of the text is to provide (1) a basic system within which students may find guidelines for the development of logical thinking related to ethical decisions or actions in matters affecting human conduct in the teaching and administration of physical education and in the coaching or administration of sport; (2) a framework of reference based on substantive theoretical data to be used as a context to guide thinking which is logical, meet criteria for objective and well-grounded judgments, and permit conclusions or decisions to be arrived at in a consequential manner; and (3) a presentation and treatment of selected prominent incidents which comprise major categories of ethical concern to the profession.

The contents of the text emphasize normative ethics with a supporting base of principles that issue from recognized but selected ethical theories. This approach to study should be helpful to readers of the text as they are confronted in their professional and personal lives in making decisions or taking actions in both contemporary times and in the decades of the future.

It is intended that the ethical study experience provided by the text as one means toward helping students to make decisions will assist in cultivating independence of thought and action through practice in applying criteria of moral judgment. The central problem of ethics is the shaping of ethical standards in the form of answers to the questions, What should (ought) I do? What are the grounds on which we can say of any action, or any ethical principle, that it is right or wrong? What makes right actions right? What reasons can be given for saying that an action or decision or principle is right?

The text will assist students to find the answers to such questions in the absence of indoctrination. The classroom environment is one of interchange of value experiences through study and discussion which (1) revolves around carefully described ethical incidents and (2) is structured through the application of a disciplined method which assists in the development of ethical perspectives.

The ethical incident in physical education and sport represents the major source out of which one arrives at ethical judgments. The incident approach serves as a simple yet well-constructed manner of synchronizing a validated method for ethical reasoning and principle construction. Thus the principle construction process is inductive rather than deductive.

The entire process of applying a validated method to ethical incidents in physical education and sport should enable students to *cultivate* an open-mindedness toward values held by others, to *clarify* their own thoughts and feelings, to *challenge* them to consider all possible alternatives and their consequences within a criteria list of rightness, and to *confront* them with a need for decision making based upon their own sense of personal and social values.

Both teacher and student will find the sections on Discussion Topics and Ethical Incidents, which are included at the end of each chapter, to be especially interesting and helpful. They comprise, in many instances, actual ethical incidents which have existed in practical day-to-day situations. These sections are intended to be relevant to the reader's interest because they reflect contemporary problems and conflicts brought about by shifts in recent thought and practices. The ethical incidents stated are varied in nature. Although placed within a context of physical education and sport, they are related to many of the larger issues which confront society. For example, incidents are presented which involve pornography, homosexuality, corporal punishment, human rights, individual privilege, racial discrimination, sport as a business, alienation, and drug abuse.

Additionally, the bibliography contains a listing of supplementary readings. Among these are a mixture of the older, traditional, but basic expressions of ethical principles which are found in the great systems of moral philosophy of the past (at least one of which every student might read) and the contemporary up-to-date publications which reflect proposed adjustments and applications of ethical theory in an attempt to be more relevant for the decades which lie ahead.

Support for the Text

There are several reasons for producing a text which provides an ethical study experience in physical education and sport. These are as follows:

1. Courses on principles of physical education have been highly influenced by the sciences of physiology of exercise and work (including physical fitness), kinesiology, motor learning, biomechanics, educational psychology, psychology and sociology of sport, and psychology. Surveys of the contents of texts on principles of physical education indicate that, while some provision is included for the areas of curriculum, methodology, administration, and evaluation, the primary bases or sources for principles issue from the basic and applied sciences.

The curricula for the professional preparation of physical educators who also coach sport have been considerably strengthened in recent years so as to include *specific* courses in the basic and applied sciences while continuing the traditionally offered courses on evaluation, administration, curriculum, methodology, and in many instances, the history of physical education. The content of the present type of course on principles of physical education is apt, therefore, to become repetitious of the knowledges and understandings acquired in the specific course or subject matter areas. It is expected that the interrelationships between such knowledges and their applications of physical education can be made meaningful within the specific applied science courses, by the student, or in other traditional courses which deal with the application of theory (administration, curriculum methodology, evaluation).

There has been little or no provision in the curriculum of professional education for moral philosophy, ethical theory, or ethics related to the teaching of physical education and coaching.

2. Physical education has long considered the development of desirable standards of human behavior (conduct) as one of its prominent objectives. The objective has been indicated in a variety of ways. Representative titles often refer to it as social development, ethical character, sportsmanship, sociopsychological values, social and moral standards of behavior, moral development, and spiritual and moral strength, among others. Teachers and coaches highly subscribe to the importance of the development of social and moral values through competitive sports and games. Their printed professional codes highly support these values. The very nature of the environment of physical education and sport, they state, is one which stimulates the emotions of participants under circumstances in which the rules of the game direct conduct toward goals which are consistent with the type of behavior which is expected of good citizens in a democratic society. Under the proper type of educational leadership, physical education and athletics offer a splendid opportunity for teaching desirable standards of human conduct.

Conversely, there are ample opportunities for participants to learn undesirable forms of behavior. Research only feebly supports the contention that sports and games always develop desirable ethical values. There is little or no evidence that the ethical and moral values learned, and practices in physical education and sport will transfer to life in general. These facts do not and should not deter the teacher and coach from strongly supporting attempts to aid in the realization of the objective.

The point to be made is that the objective of physical education and competitive sport related to the development of desirable standards of ethical and moral conduct is worthy. This text highly supports this objective and attempts in a specific way to substantially contribute to its realization.

3. Significant changes have occurred in the personal and interpersonal lives of people in a relatively short time, many of which have created strong influences on human thought and conduct. These changes have been brought about largely by events of a national and international nature and issue from the political, economic, social, and military spheres of endeavor. They represent responses to one of the most challenging problems the world can face between now and the end of the twentieth century, namely, the description of humanistic relations between people and their environment. The increase of impersonal, urban-industrial systems and lack of moral idealism with an obsession of material benefits may substantially contribute to this enormous problem.

Each generation grows up in relation to the social, physical, and intellectual environment of its time, and its values are fashioned by it. Changes in the environment produce events that cause people to reorder an existing sense of values. The individual has become the focus of concern and, through introspection, reflects a hierarchy of values in which personal values are given highest priority. The emphasis on the individual with increased freedom of expression, action, and decision making is seen to be demonstrated in ways of living, dress styles, the manner of participation in the controversial issues of the times, human mobility, communication interchange, and personal modes of behavior, among others. Individuals more prominently make their decisions about personal involvement in life's affairs as they see the relevancy of such affairs to their own lives.

These types of changes have been reflected in education as seen in movements of individualization and humanization of instructional techniques, in the increased or continued participation of the individual in physical education based upon recognized relevancy to interests and motivations, to decreases in compulsory participation in formalized programs, and to wide-spread adjustments in curricula, methods of teaching, teacher preparation, and administrative procedures.

Since changes in human minds and lives have occurred rather rapidly, one must be concerned about the ethical problems associated with changes in behavior and life patterns of endeavor. It is impossible to disassociate or remove the decisions or actions taken by human beings in periods of extensive adjustments which affect their personal lives from an ethical and moral context in which all such decisions or actions properly reside. Yet, it would seem that one of the primary causes of the difficulties confronted by humanity has been the failure to fully consider and apply well-tested principles of ethical and moral action not only in relation to the effects on the individual but upon all of the universal life.

Human capacity for intelligently directed self-development provides the ability to determine future patterns to the culture and environment and thus shape the course of human events in the direction of one's own choice. This ability, which no other animal has, is humanity's most distinctive characteristic. The choice of decision within a moral and ethical context of human values may decide fundamental changes in human nature and significantly alter the destiny of all humankind.

CONTENTS

Ethical Decisions
in Physical Education
and Sport

All human beings are born free and equal in dignity and rights. They are endowed with reason and conscience and should act towards one another in a spirit of brotherhood.

United Nations General Assembly
Universal Declaration of Human Rights

The overriding problem today is to arrive at an ultimate common denominator in the world — a denominator which would reconcile the conflicts of material goods and social ideals and suppress forever the destructive forces which are now delicately balanced in intense rivalry against each other.

The ultimate common denominator, and the point at which all conflicting interests ultimately converge, is man.

Moses Moskowitz
Human Rights and World Order

The development of moral and spiritual values is basic to all other educational objectives. Education uninspired by moral and spiritual values is directionless. Values unapplied in human behavior are empty.

Educational Policies Commission of the
National Education Association
*Moral and Spiritual Values in the
Public Schools*

Chapter 1

ETHICS AND DECISIONS IN PHYSICAL EDUCATION AND SPORT

THE need to search for clarity in one's beliefs about the nature of right and wrong conduct, as well as to better provide a philosophical basis for decision making in the field of physical education and sport, is important. The degree of interaction is often intense between participants and competitors in an environment where the emotions are raised to high levels and where both function within a context of rules and regulations which attempt to bring behavior into line with ethical principles. The physical education environment provides excellent opportunities to apply ethical deliberations in an effort to better determine whether conduct may be considered as right or wrong, good or bad.

In this respect, the classroom of physical education and sport considerably differs from that of the conventional classroom. The very nature of the subject matter content is that of physical movement or that which revolves around physical movement designed to achieve cognitive, effective, psychomotor, and tactical purposes. Physical education teachers and athletic coaches have steadfastly adhered to the conviction that participation in such an environment, when operating under good educational leadership, a sound educational philosophy, and good administrative practices, yields values supportive of the qualities of character and citizenship. The development of desirable standards of human conduct has always remained a prominent educational objective of physical education.

Whether or not participants in the physical education and sport experience acquire and further develop such qualities and are capable of interpreting standards of good conduct within the context of total life is left for other fields of academic endeavor. Our concern here is one of the study of the relationship between ethics and decision making in the process of con-

3

ducting one's behavior in physical education and sport.

THE MEANING OF ETHICS

Ethics attempts to answer the question "Why?" in instances that involve acts that may be judged to be right or wrong, good or bad. There may be a number of different answers to this question, and the answers must be judged as to their value. Since ethics deal with value judgments, and the validity of value judgments is subjected to scrutiny, the most adequate answer is sought to the question, What makes decisions or actions right or wrong?

It is, for example, the practice in sport that participants realize the outcome of good sportsmanship as a result of the training and competitive experience. Sportsmanship represents a characteristic found among the moral ideals that exist within a broad social context in which we live and is related to the behavioral pattern and philosophical beliefs of citizens in a democratic society. Among other such ideals are the respect of human dignity, tolerance, understanding others (particularly those unlike oneself), loyalty toward group welfare, fair play, cooperation, support of others, and sacrifice of self for the welfare of others.

That these characteristics are not always demonstrated in action in the competitive sport scene or that such beliefs are not fully supported by some athletes has been particularly noted in recent years. Since competitive sport experience also attempts to develop such qualities as self-reliance, initiative, leadership, aggressiveness, and self-confidence, the question arises, Is it possible to develop the quality of aggressive leadership under competitive conditions within a framework of rules and regulations which are tempered by the golden rule of sportsmanship? Out of this environment emerges opportunities for ethical studies.

Values of Sport Often Questioned

The values recognized as worthy outcomes of the sport or physical education experience are sometimes questioned as to nature and degree. For example, the concept of amateurism in a democratic culture has, in modern times, undergone extreme criticism. The adherence of the concept to the ideal that training and participation in competitive sport should exist as an avocation in the spirit of play for the inherent values for the individual athlete not seeking financial and subsistence support in the process has been claimed as outdated. The original intention to protect and preserve the values of true amateurism has been indicated as inconsistent with modern day thinking. True amateurism, it has been stated, exists in an environment where the game or contest serves as a *means* of permitting the individual to best realize realistic educational and personal values. Governmental support for the athlete, such as provided in communistic or other societies, places the individual in a position where he or she serves as the *means* of winning the contest, with winning becoming the *end* rather than the means.

Do athletes really make extensive sacrifices for the welfare of the team? Do they engage in fair play? Cooperation? Loyalty toward group welfare? Does the team or group or country come first, or does the individual come first in terms of social approval, notoriety, and personal aggrandizement?

A most prominent, former amateur athlete in the United States stated, "To hell with love of country, I compete for myself." Frustrated because of the financial disadvantages of the American athletes compared to athletes from other parts of the world, he stated, "I'm the one who made all the sacrifices; those are *my* American records, not the country's" (italics added). This same type of thinking often permeates society at large. An elected official in public affairs stated, "I was taught to deal with the world on two levels. One set of values were for those in your family. Within the family, you were to have love and respect and mutual caring. But my parents said to me, 'If you stick by these values in the real world, you're going to get kicked in the ass. The world doesn't operate like that, and you have to know it.'"

A Description of Ethics

We judge that conduct such as sportsmanship is not only

Figure 1. The fundamental element in ethical relationships is the human character. (Photo courtesy of the *Denver Post*.)

expected in the games and sports of physical education but that it is also right, that to deviate from it is wrong, and that it results from some abiding principle in a person's own convictions of a sense of wrongness and rightness. This type of conduct deals with morals, and it is with these that ethics deals. Hence, ethics is the study of right and wrong, of good and bad, in human conduct.

While ethics is concerned with the problems of right and wrong in human conduct, it is best demonstrated in practice through the application of techniques of ethical inquiry and critical intelligence. It includes the shaping of moral standards and seeks, on an individual basis, to answer the question, What should (ought) I do?

While it is not an express description of moral standards, ethics is concerned with discovering standards in accordance with which conduct may be judged good or bad. Thus it is a normative rather than a descriptive science. It seeks to tell us not what *is*, but what *ought* to be. It is concerned with facts as they support one's hypothesis relating to human values, but it is more concerned with the moral values themselves. In this sense ethics is more concerned with the ends or goals of living rather than the means of living. Whenever we think about the ultimate good toward which any type of human activity is directed, we are in the field of ethics.

What are the ultimate purposes of competitive sport? Does sport exist for the individual, or does the individual serve as a means to further the end of winning the contest? Is winning the *only* thing? What should be or ought to be the *only* objective in sport competition?

Since ethics is so concerned with values, one can easily understand the degree of involvement of the moral dimension of the subject. For this reason, ethics is often indicated as the philosophy of morality. It is that branch of philosophy which critically examines, clarifies, and reframes the basic concepts and presuppositions of morality in general. It makes clear to us why one act is better than another. From what has already been pointed out, we may say that, in a more specific way, ethics attempts to abstract, clarify, and examine the ideas of good and bad, right or wrong.

This latter process is referred to as ethical theory, as contrasted to ethical practice. Here we are concerned not with the kinds of actions that ought to be performed or what is right or wrong, but rather what is meant by these terms where we apply them. In this sense, ethics may be divided into two divisions: (1) practical ethics concerned with the kinds of actions as right and wrong, good or bad, and (2) ethical theory (referred to as meta-ethics) concerned with the meaning of the terms right or wrong, good or bad. This latter division of treatment will be presented in a succeeding chapter.

WHY STUDY ETHICS IN PHYSICAL EDUCATION?

A person may ask, "What need have I of an ethics-study experience? I already know the do's and don'ts of right and wrong conduct. And I know what good sportsmanship is and the rules of the games. Why spend time on studying this material?"

If one feels that he or she can progress through the physical education and competitive sport experience armed with only such a preparation, the results may be frustrating. Ethical questions will involve more than a knowledge of games rules or rules of behavioral conduct. Other persons will continually challenge such rules or state other rules which contradict one's own. One must be capable of justifying the acceptance of rules if they are satisfactory or their rejection if they are not satisfactory. Such explanations may transcend only the immediate instance in which rules are to be applied.

Even philosophers in the field of meta-ethics, wherein investigations are conducted into the meaning of ethical statements and clarification and justifications of ethical theories, continue to raise the question as to whether or not this process makes any real difference in the contemporary expressions of moral codes and moral attitudes. It is often argued that such a process need not affect the actual use of moral concepts and that a person's actions and attitudes remain unaltered by meta-ethical considerations.

We often hear such statements as, "Mr. Brown should not neglect his teaching as he does in order to spend more time on his athletic coaching." "Miss Green was doing her duty when she insisted that students in physical education adhere to the rules of proper dress while in class." "Johnny is a good football player, but his character is bad." "Jane ought not to have demonstrated poor sportsmanship behavior when losing." These kinds of statements are sometimes subject to disagreement among parents, spectators, athletes, and sports fans. The basis for differences in opinions concerning such statements or judgments rests upon one's meanings of good or bad, right or wrong. Agreement is seldom possible on such judgments until the meanings of such terms are clarified. There are many other questions which arise out of an attempt to seek clarification, but basically the effort to do so constitutes the type of study experience with which ethics deals.

Will Ethics-Study Make a Person Better?

There is no assurance that a person who understands by means of ethical-study the difference between right and wrong will necessarily follow the right. The study of moral decisions will not in itself make a person more or less moral. It has often been indicated that examples of moral behavior demonstrated by good educational leadership in the form of the teacher of physical education and sport are likely to be more effective influences in producing good conduct than simply the reading-study experience alone. People who study ethics are no more nor less apt to cheat, lie, take unfair advantage of the opponents, or break the rules than those who do not study the subject. The physician or health educator does not necessarily follow proper health practices.

It is reasonable to expect, however, that a knowledge of ethics will provide some assistance in the pursuit of rightness and goodness even if by way of casuistry. It is also reasonable to expect that a person who has studied the ethical dimensions of the physical education and sport experience is more apt to be less biased and more flexible and comprehensive in applying moral concepts to a particular case than a person who, while knowing the circumstances, has little or no knowledge of ethics. But even from a more general view, and apart from a specific case, a knowledge of ethical principles and their supporting theory should better prepare a person to deal with situations involving moral matters.

One should not expect that upon completing a study of ethical decisions he or she will be equipped with a rule-of-thumb technique which may be applied in an automatic way and thereby be capable of solving all ethical problems. Even in situations which are quite similar in nature, there are always circumstances which require a flexible approach in reaching decisions and taking action. The study of ethics, however, should provide a more sophisticated insight into the nature of morality and could enable the student, if he or she desires, to make more adequate decisions.

It is not the intention of this text to make people better but to understand ethical behavior and provide the experience of constructing principles and standards to guide ethical conduct. Ethics seeks a body of truth about morals. The chief objective is to cause the student to reflect on moral situations in order to answer questions about them.

Characteristics of an Ethical Problem

The following example will help to clarify some of the characteristics of an ethical problem in physical education.

The entire area of academic eligibility which requires students to meet established standards of academic performance in order to represent their school or college in extracurricular or out-of-class events offers many examples of decision making related to ethical conduct. In this specific example, the head basketball coach of a middle-size high school is also a teacher of mathematics. The practice in the state high school association which governs the conduct of athletics requires the filing of eligibility certificates on each athlete each week. The basketball captain and all-state nominee has been doing poorly in math and failed the most recent math test and will, on grade reports, go ineligible for the first game of the state tournament. The player's father, who is also chairperson of the school board, visits the coach and cites the importance of the state championship to the school and the community, but he applies no pressure. Nevertheless, the implication of personal consequences is obvious. The grades are scheduled to be filed the afternoon of the morning visit from the school board chairperson. The student, of course, is aware of his or her status.

The questions that must be asked which indicate the characteristics of this ethical problem are, What alternatives are there in terms of what ought to be the decision or action? Can the alternatives, if any, be tested against criteria of what is right? (It may be that any suggested alternative will fail at this point.) What will be the probable consequences of each of the alternatives in terms of the effects on those most immediately involved, on the thoughts, feelings, and responses of others, and on the moral standards of the school and community? After comparing the probable consequences of each alternative, which one, if any, will be selected that best proves most valid and indicates consequences which will lead to the best course of action in terms of what is right?

Thus, it may be seen that raising ethical questions should improve deliberation on difficult decisions to be made in situations where alternate actions may be taken or where there are debatable choices involving the question or morals. Such questions may serve as direction-finders enabling the deliberations to focus on the matter of relative values, not only in relation to absolute right or wrong, but values to be considered on the basis of their relative worth on priority listing. Persons without the ethics-study experience may otherwise fail to include the use of ethical deliberations in as logical and comprehensive a manner as might be possible.

Application to Program

The ethics-study experience should also assist one who participates in the formation or application of principles, policies, and rules as they affect a number of important components in the total physical education program, such as personnel, facilities, curricula, equipment use, and program development or adjustments.

Examples of the application of ethical questions that might be raised relative to their effects on important components of the total physical education program are, What criteria should be established for the employment of teachers of physical education who must also coach competitive sports? How steadfast should one hold to the criteria when considering the employment of a much-needed coach or a major sport who has been an All-American with a record of coaching success, when at the same time there exists an urgent need for a teacher of kinesiology or physiology of exercise? What guidelines should be used when considering an applicant who is a relative or a close friend? To what degree should limited facilities be shared between girls and boys in both physical education instructional classes and athletic team practice? Should all school events or spectator sports events, or public relation or public entertainment events receive priority in facility scheduling over academic (physical education) classes? To what degree should the utilization of teaching services of coaches of sport be made in a climate of (1) intense efforts to achieve a status of *number one* in the athletic world with its commensurate reward system and (2) a status of high academic achievement which seeks its rewards under its own criteria for research, teaching, and service? Should students be excused from the instructional program of physical education for participation in such programs as athletics, cheerleading, pompon team, and band membership for the reason that these programs require physical activity and exercise?

The ethics-study experience should also provide both a theoretical and practical experience for rational analysis development for those who may, as part of their functions, express judgment upon the actions and decisions of others. This type of experience may particularly refer to those who perform in administrative positions and evaluate the performance of others for purposes of salary increases, promotions, and tenure.

Need for Review of Principles and Facts

It has been indicated many times that no past decision or old policies and old principles can be totally relied upon to justify a present course of action. Policies which serve the purpose of assisting one to be consistent in taking action or in making decisions in situations which are quite similar and which have been formulated and tested over a long period of time need to be reviewed and tested by ethical questions or theories. This approach is also needed in the application of rules and regulations which apply to specific situations. This is true because each case needs to be tested in light of its own circumstances which surround it. There are nearly always exceptions or exceptional circumstances which apply, if not to the total situation, then to parts of it, which may influence final decisions. One does not apply hunches or gut-feelings to situations which involve the welfare of individuals or institutions as if it were the same as selecting a fast horse at a race track.

There is wisdom which, when applied, can save one from blind trial-and-error judgment. This wisdom is that which issues from the application of ethical standards based upon a knowledge and understanding of sound ethical theory related to consistency with principle, awareness of prejudices, affects on happiness, obligation, duty, rights, justice, intention or motive, choice, responsibility, and rightness.

It is not expected that the ethics-study experience can provide ready-made solutions to all situations. Often, only tentative hypotheses are warranted. The element of some trial and error from practical decisions is sometimes difficult to eliminate even with the soundest of formulated principles or policies. Neither is there any assurance that the ethics-study experience will produce the wise practitioner, the ethical performer, or the prudent judge.

Finally, it may be pointed out that the entire process of searching for clearness and cogency in one's beliefs about the nature of right and wrong conduct does involve a supportive base in facts if we are to deal with the truth. The collection and consideration of facts in situations where decisions are to be made are very important. But the consideration of facts in the absence of relative values of the consequences can be a serious mistake. Those who express good judgment are most often those who weigh the value considerations. Thoughtless or compulsive conduct is thus avoided.

While fact gathering constitutes an important part of decision making, it should be noted that even after the facts are available, one must be guided by standards or principles which have logical meaning, are acceptable, and, when applied, provide direction for decisions which may be interpreted as good or right. The interpretation of these latter terms, good and right, constitutes the primary focus on which the philosophical inquiry in ethics is directed.

What is the nature of these principles? How shall we construct adequate and acceptable statements of principles? The next chapter, *A Method of Ethical Judgment and Principle Construction,* will attempt to answer these questions.

DECISION MAKING

Definition and Characteristics

There are certain ingredients which comprise the recognition of a decision-making situation. While these are logically recognizable, the intervention of ethical considerations would seem to be necessary, particularly in situations which involve the welfare of the decision maker or others. Ignizia and Gupta[12] indicate that the general requirements which lead to motivating the making of a decision are as follows: a decision maker, a problem, the recognition of the problem by the decision maker, a need or pressure to alleviate or eliminate the problem, more than one feasible action (alternative), and an uncertainty of which action is best. It is at the point of a choice to be made from alternatives that we are concerned. It aids us to more clearly define a decision as *making a judgment in relation to what one ought to do in a certain situation after having deliberated on some alternative courses of action.* This implies there are choices and that individuals are free to make their own choice. The best case for the individual as far as freedom of choice is concerned exists where the individual is confronted with a choice-situation, deliberates and compares different possibilities, and finally makes the judgment that one ought to act in a specifically described manner.

While all of the elements indicated are related to a decision-making situation, they may or may not involve the types of alternatives which embrace ethics. For example, what are the alternatives to the punt returner in football while he waits to catch the ball in flight as the opposition thunders down upon him; or to the goaltender in field hockey or ice hockey while waiting for the penalty shot to be fired; or to the third baseman in baseball who realizes the dire need for the double play; or when in-bounding the basketball at midcourt with three seconds to play and with one point behind? The performer in the fast-moving action of play must make rapid decisions, none of which, however, may be related to value judgments. The decisions related to tactical actions which are responsible for improved team or individual performance, because they are tactical, may be executed in the absence of moral and ethical principles.

However, suppose that, on a preplanned arrangement, the player fakes an injury in the last half-minute of the contest so as to stop the clock and gain time for an extra play or two. While the player may be lost to the team and while no letter of the rule has been abridged, the matter of the spirit of the rules, and hence ethical behavior, is involved. Here we have an additional element which is injected into the decision-making process which is critical in transforming action from one which is purely tactical in nature to one which is ethical, since the matter of ethical and moral judgments may be involved.

Relation of Decision Making to Ethics

Decisions or guidelines for human actions formed from value judgments related to what should be or what one ought to do which affect the lives of people are invariably related to the field of ethics. Thus, we indicate that principles are statements of truth which issue from scientific facts or moral action based on philosophical concepts and theories which, when applied, serve as guides in making decisions or taking actions in situations which involve the education and/or welfare of people. Since our concern here is with decisions which are to be based upon philosophical considerations, one can readily discern the relationship with ethics. Ethics is concerned with standards of conduct, that is, actions of a voluntary nature based upon decisions which have been formed out of a weighing of values which involve the welfare of the individual and groups, or society. Ethics asks what kind of acts are right or wrong, good or bad, or ought or ought not to be done, and what these terms mean.

It is important to note that, in most of the behavior responses which are to be cited in this text, conduct as viewed within the concept of ethical behavior is conditioned by the factor of voluntary activity. Very seldom is conduct dictated from an external source, but instead it results from the individual's decision. The emphasis here on the word *voluntary* is very important. It is on the point of voluntary action based on decision making or choosing from alternative courses of action that our primary interests lie. We think of a voluntary action as one in which a person could have responded differently if he or she had so chosen. It includes all willed or volitional actions in which persons have conscious control over their actions. It is in this realm of human conduct and decision making that our interest in physical education and sport resides.

Much consideration has been given to decision theory and its evaluation, but most treatments have been provided by mathematicians and economists, providing little, if any, information on ethical relations to the process and consequences of decision making. Economists seem more concerned with decisions which result in maximum profits or material usefulness and less with the ethics of human behavior. Mathematicians are more concerned with mathematical theory of decision making and are little concerned with ethical consequences of human choice. Yet, human choices and related conduct have been based upon a variety of sources, such as reason, duty, instinct, reinforcement, altruism, custom, law, group approval, and conscience, among others.

There has been, of recent years, a tendency to place more reliance upon a base of feeling, self-expression, and individual interpretation of a personal nature rather than duty, reason, instinct, etc., in arriving at decisions. Whatever the approach to decision making and whatever actions follow which involve human behavior that affect the life of the decision maker or lives of others, the inclusion in the process of ethical considerations represents a worthy endeavor.

Decisional Conflicts

Not all decision making concludes in a satisfactory and acceptable manner for the decision maker. When choosing between at least two things that one values equally, a person may experience two kinds of conflict. These conflicts are described by Casteel and Stahl[4] as (1) predecision conflict and (2) postdecision dissonance. The first conflict results from not being able to make a completely satisfactory choice. The person experiences an internal struggle because of having to choose one alternative at the expense of surrendering another. One surrenders the benefits that would have been received had the choice been different, while having to accept negative consequences which accompany the decision made.

The second conflict is characterized by doubt and regret which follows the making of the decision. One tends to view the negative consequences of the chosen alternative and weigh them against the possible positive and desirable consequences of the alternatives that were rejected. When one experiences doubt and regret of the decision that was made, dissonance results.

These types of decisional conflicts are typical of those which are experienced by coaches, players, and fans after a closely contested event which results in a loss or a tie. The selection by the coach of the wrong relief pitcher or pinch hitter, the calling of the wrong play in a critical situation, the submission to the officials of an alternative line-up, the employment of a less-successful coach, the utterance of a published remark, the recruitment of an athlete who meets less than projected expectations, the choice of a wrong golf club, the failure to follow a preplanned running pace — all may be typical examples of commonly experienced conflict situations. The Monday morning quarterback fan meetings represent expressions of criticism of coach and player decisions and postdecision dissonance. These types of decisional conflicts are not uncommon among teachers of physical education and school administrators.

Predecision conflict and postdecision dissonance are often accentuated when one is brought to the point of decision making in an environment of isolation. One is less apt to experience such conflicts when able to share and articulate with others the analysis and comparative evaluation of the consequences of alternatives and to test the reasonableness of a choice. Casteel and Stahl present a rather fatalistic view by stating, "Unless one learns to resolve predecision conflict and to cope with postdecision dissonance, he may refuse to acknowledge that a decision needs to be made and, in extreme cases, may argue that his freedom and skill are irrelevant. In effect, he comes to believe that fate controls his actions and determines his experiences, and he no longer perceives himself as a responsible agent in human affairs" (p. 3).

Types of Decision Theories

There are two general types of decision theory processes. Of the two types, *normative* decision theory would seem to have a particular relationship to the application of ethical theories in arriving at decisions. Normative decision theory is concerned with the choices that a person *should* make in a particular situation, regardless of the choices that persons actually make. *Descriptive* decision theory concerns the choices persons actually make, regardless of the choices they should make.

For example, whether it involves Mary as a member of the girls' varsity basketball team or Jimmie as a member of the varsity football team, both very clearly understand the rules of training established by the coach. All team members have readily accepted the rules and agree to abide by them because they are motivated by the common objective of having a successful season. The rules which govern their conduct off the field of play require self-discipline not only because the individual is more apt to benefit in terms of improved performance in the game, but also because, collectively, the team will benefit. The individual is thus willing to make sacrifices in order that the team better achieve its goal.

Mary or Jimmie is discovered in the lounge of the local theatre by several teammates to have violated the nonsmoking rule, a practice whose penalty is dismissal from the team. Normative description theory does not stop at the point of decisions made by the three decision makers in this instance: the coach, the team members, and the athlete. An exposition of normative theories applicable to each decision-making element would easily reveal alternate possibilities. Most likely, the decisions would have been different. The coach might have stopped short of invoking the dismissal penalty and instead offered guidance, the team members might have exerted peer pressure rather than inform the coach, and the athlete might never have violated the rules' provision.

Observation and experience related to both normative and descriptive decision theories has led to the hypothesis that, generally, people *do* make the decisions they *should* make. In this sense the theories tend to merge in actual practice.

DECISION MAKING IN AN ETHICAL CONTEXT

Long-term Decision Making

The primary purpose of considering decision making in an ethical context is to assist in making wise decisions within a normative or descriptive framework. Of course, one of the best means of evaluating the worth of decisions is to judge the resultant actions that have been taken after a period of time and to judge whether or not such actions proved to be ethically wise ones. Thus the consequences of the actions and the additional time to reflect upon ethical values can permit one to form more valid judgments concerning the worth of the decision. This type of decision making implies that there will be a length of time available to perform reflective thinking in order to compare consequences and decisively choose the better course of action.

This longer-term type of thinking which precedes decisions or conclusions made within the context of ethical deliberations is not as firmly or objectively structured as is that which derives from easily definable sciences. This, to a large extent, is due to the framework within which thinking is directed. A contrast between the steps which direct progress in the scientific method and the application of logic in ethical deliberations makes this point very clear.

We may indicate the scientific method procedure as follows:

1. The truth of a scientific proposition is established by logical and empirical methods. It is explicit, self-correcting, and the results are verifiable.
2. It is objective and does not depend upon vested interests or personalities or a diversity of moral postulations of individuals or groups.
3. Each hypothesis is tested and verified by methods appropriate to it — logically, experimentally, historically, or in other ways.
4. The quantitative components are often dominant, that is, clearness in progress and thought are achieved by using quantitative data or numbers and are treated quantitatively.

It should be noted that the scientific method does not exclude judgment and insight which can be very useful when applied in a logical and well-structured manner.

The steps involved in the application of logical deduction based upon reflective thinking are not quite as precise. (We shall consider this particular process in more detail in the next chapter dealing with a method of ethical thinking and application to the physical education and sport situation.) A contrasting view of the scientific method might be described as follows:

1. Logical, ethical deduction involves a systematic approach to aid a decision maker choose a course of action by thoughtfully considering all objectives and alternatives through reflective thinking and comparing them in the light of their consequences for good or bad, right or wrong, as expressed in the acts which follow such decisions.
2. The framework through which such reflective thinking is performed is dialectic and analytic in nature in order to bring judgment fully influenced by ethical theory to bear upon the problem. One strives to consider the total problem, which requires decision judgments, and to compare alternative choices in light of the ethical outcomes.

An example of decision making in an ethical context under conditions in which there is time to apply a method of reflective thinking and logical deduction may be cited: The 200-meter runner has been informed by several members of the track team that the ingestion of amphetamines prior to a race will improve the runner's performance, create a feeling of exhilaration and general well-being, and generate more physical power. As the time for the conference championship approaches, the runner who possesses a strong desire to finish his or her sport career with a conference victory ponders the advice of teammates. Apart from the questions of the effects of drugs upon the physiological and mental functions of the body, the important questions of ethics, of what is morally right or wrong, remain to be considered.

Short-term Decision Making

There is, in contrast to the longer-term type of reflective thinking and decision making, a type of decision process which occurs within a very brief period of time and is devoid of the possibilities of applying a method or system of deliberation. This decision process has been partly described by Hegel[10] who pointed out that there is a perpetual and unbridgeable gap between thought and action in the domain of ethics which is often a source of despair. Often, within that gap lies an intense drama enacted between the hostility of forces that exist both in the conditions of life and in the constitution of the individual person. It can be the fragment of life within which a person faces a crisis of moral isolation and recognition and in which one meets a full test of character in the struggle between conscience and desire. It is characterized by the person who, having been brought to the edge of decision making, must act in such a way that the consequences may well decide his or her future destiny. It is seen in the situation faced by Conrad's Lord Jim as he stood at the rail of the Patna, faced with the ethical decision as to whether or not to jump and abandon ship, leaving 800 humans at the mercy of an extreme squall at sea. It is characterized by many of the prominent personages in the literature of history whose decisions involved both their personal lives and the lives of others. It is characterized by those caught up in the web of unresolved moral problems, never finding peace within themselves, always confronted with the possibilities of failure or condemnation and constantly living in the existential climate of anguish and despair.

The performer in sport often is confronted with having to make decisions which are related to actions outside of the letter and spirit of the rules but which also may contribute to a winning performance. Consider, for example, the defensive lineman who quickly moves into the offensive backfield to find a clear shot at the blind side of the quarterback who is attempting to release the ball. The defensive player suddenly becomes aware of (1) the open exposure of the quarterback now vulnerable from the side to injury from an extremely hard tackle, and (2) an opportunity to inflict an injury which would terminate the quarterback's further play in that game (and possibly succeeding games), thus improving the chances for a win for the team of the defensive player.

This brief-period type of decision making in an ethical context by the participant in sport often reveals his or her true character. It cannot be hidden from others because overt actions

Figure 2. Short-term decision making by the defensive lineman. In the gap between thought and action in the domain of ethics there often lies an intense drama enacted among the hostility of forces that exist in the struggle between conscience and desire.

reflect the decisions of the participant often within an atmosphere of intense interaction between humans.

Ethics as a Source of Guidance in Decision Making

The entire process of ethical thinking — that is, the application of ethical theory — produces no assurance of the rightness or wrongness of specific decisions, but it is certain to contribute to the process of arriving at decisions involving the type of conduct which follows. It should enable the decision maker to see and to weigh evidence prior to action and the values which are affected by specific decisions.

How does one establish a relationship between ethics and decision making? That there is a relationship between standards of ethics and the controversial issues of our public and private lives is clear. One need only to examine some of the prime issues that confront our society, such as abortion, euthanasia, premarital sex, decriminalizing marijuana, bussing, homosexuals as school teachers, and capital punishment.

The same relationship exists between ethics and the immediate issues in physical education and sport. The high school basketball coach who teaches mathematics must make a moral decision related to the grade eligibility of his or her poorly academic performing captain to play in the opening game of the state tournament.

The point of importance is that with the establishment of relations between decision making and questions of ethical theory, it is possible to arrive at decisions in such a way as to exclude visceral or gut feelings or emotions and hunches and to bring to bear upon the thinking of the decision maker or makers more enlightened thought based on ethical principle.

Whether or not ethics can be relied upon as a valid and reliable source for guidance and direction in decision making will, in large measure, depend upon the decision maker's ability to (1) construct and comprehend a framework of ethical theories which can be applied to the situation on hand, (2) determine the degree of relevancy of specific ethical theories to the situation, and (3) formulate decisions on the basis of synthesis or relationships between ethics and the situation. The entire process is, in this text, presented as a method of ethical judgment, a method which permits the formulation of standards or principles which provide the direction for decisions and actions.

DISCUSSION TOPICS AND ETHICAL INCIDENTS

1. What three conditions do physical education teachers and

coaches of sport feel are essential if participation in sports and games are to yield qualities of good ethical conduct and behavior? (p. 3.)

2. Explain why ethics as presented and applied in this text is a normative rather than a descriptive science. Apply your answer to the *ends* as contrasted to the *means* for which competitive sport should exist (p. 7.)

3. Why is it that a thorough knowledge of the rules of sports and games, in themselves, are not sufficient in explaining human conduct? One does not for example, pile up on a downed opponent after the whistle has blown. What are some of the reasons behind the rules of sport? For example, a pitcher is not permitted to intentionally throw the ball at a batter; a defensive player is not permitted to make contact with the quarterback once the ball has been released and the arm is no longer in a forward motion; a basketball defensive player is not permitted to run under a player who is suspended in air at the height of a jump while shooting.

4. Is it likely that a person who understands the difference between right and wrong will necessarily follow the right? In what ways might the ethical study experience positively influence decisions and actions in cases which involve the question of ethical behavior in physical education and sport? (p. 9.)

5. Why should one not expect that a rule-of-thumb approach to applying principles to all ethical incidents will work even though the incidents might seem similar? Why should each incident be tested in light of its own circumstances which surround it? (p. 10.)

6. Provide an example of a situation in sport and physical education in which decision making may be devoid of ethical considerations; provide an example of a situation in which decision making *is* related to ethics. What are the factors in each type of situation which distinguish between whether or not decision making is related to ethics? (p. 15.)

7. Record from out of your past personal experiences or the experiences that you know of others having had in sport and physical education (1) a predecision conflict and (2) a postdecision dissonance effect (p. 17.)

8. What are the differences between the structure which directs thinking in the context of ethical deliberation as compared with the structure which directs thinking in the sciences? Contrast the steps used in the scientific method with the steps used in the application of logic in ethical deliberation. What would seem to be the important elements which cause the two methods to be different? (pp. 21-22.)

9. The defensive basketball player grasps, from behind, the jersey of the offensive player who is going up for the rebound. The officials cannot see the specific action, although a larger number of the fans do. How does this action characterize short-term decision making by the defensive player? Does it reveal the true character of the defensive player? (p. 22.)

10. Consider the following incidents for class discussion or for individual projects. Bring out all of the factors which are involved in the ethical decision-making process. Arrive at a decision concerning right or wrong in each incident and fully support the decision.

A. The most popular girl in the high school became pregnant after an affair with the most outstanding boy athlete in the high school's athletic history. The girl was president of the honor society, a recipient of a certain college scholarship awarded by the high school, and was very active in school organizations. While the athlete continued to compete for the school, the girl was dismissed from the honor society and subsequently removed from consideration for the scholarship award whose conditions included integrity and good character.

B. All competition in the Junior High School Track and Field Olympics in Johnson City is based on age. The age groups are twelve and under, thirteen years, and then fourteen- and fifteen-year-olds, and the rules require competing by age groupings. I was thirteen years of age and the fastest runner in the 120-yard low hurdles in the city. Our coach decided to take only two entrants from each age group to the J.H.S.O., and the selection of entrants for each event would be by the fastest times. Following the time trials, it was discovered that there were three thirteen-year-old hurdlers who could win this event.

However, there were no fourteen- to fifteen-year-olds who could qualify for the low hurdles or even be entered from their age group. The coach told me that he was going to enter me in the fourteen- to fifteen-year-old event because my time was fast enough to win it. Thus, the coach would have two good entries in the thriteen-year-old event who could make the trip, while at the same time helping the fourteen- to fifteen-year-old team. The coach said this action was not cheating because I would be in more difficult competition, and it was helping the team.

C. Two student athletes in a junior college were close friends, their lives being quite identical as to routines and interests. Following an auto accident, one of them was hospitalized for a period of six weeks during which an effort was made to keep up with school studies. Upon the recovered students' return to school and resumption of regular school work, it became obvious that a passing performance in one of the academic classes was borderline. As final exams approached, apprehension developed because passing the course was a necessity in order to remain eligible for fall semester sports. All students with a current grade of *A* in the course were excused from taking the final exam. (Students who had maintained regular attendance received an *A* in the course.) The student in academic difficulty approached the other and proposed that the final exam be taken by the friend as a substitute. The class was large and there would be no, or very little, probability of the substitution being detected.

D. Grade tampering for athletic eligibility purposes can take shape in a variety of forms. For example, an outstanding basketball player has difficulty in securing grades high enough to achieve academic eligibility standards. The player keeps the coach informed as to the courses which present the greatest difficulty. The coach in turn determines which teachers are susceptible to being favorably influenced toward assisting the player to maintain eligibility. The coach seeks a raising of grades from these teachers so as to offset low or failing grades from other teachers and thus permit the total grade point average (GPA) to meet eligibility standards.

E. The cry of "unfair advantage" raises on the occasion of

the entry of a transsexual into women's sport competition. The transfiguration of males who can qualify anatomically, functionally, socially, emotionally, and legally as females and compete in women's sports initiates the conflict of inequality of physical abilities. Should transsexuals be allowed to compete in women's sports? This question was raised on the event of Doctor Renee Richards, the former Doctor Richard Raskind, entering the Tennis Week Open in South Orange, New Jersey. Twenty-five of the thirty-two women entered in the tournament refused to compete if Doctor Richards was allowed to compete.

F. The conduct of sport programs in the high schools throughout the country is highly influenced by the attitudes of the people in each respective community. Those attitudes which support the need for winning that are expressed in irrational actions (fire the coach, berate the officials, harass the players, criticize the administration) often conflict with values which are consistent with educational objectives and processes. If you wanted to attempt to change the attitudes of such people toward a more constructive type of behavior, how would you go about it?

G. The behavior of parents toward their children, coaches, and officials in sport sometimes approaches serious dimensions. The Optimist Club in an active, civic-minded community was reported to have dropped its sponsorship of the basketball program for young boys and girls. The Club stated that it could no longer teach good sportsmanship while parents were such bad sports harassing referees. Officials were sometimes followed to their cars by cursing parents after the games and berated in telephone calls to their homes. The Club finally voted to suspend sponsorship of sixteen pee-wee teams on which about 180 boys and girls aged ten to thirteen years would have played.

H. The teacher of physical education who also coached two sports in the high school occupied a very important position in the minds of the young people, not only with whom the coach closely associated, but also with all others. Many important lessons of social and ethical behavior were taught by example. The opportunities for this type of teaching were limitless.

While these possibilities are always present, it is also true that the opposite effect can also occur.

For example, Coach Glass presented a figure of obesity with a large overhanging abdomen. It was common knowledge that the coach constantly smoked in the teacher's lounge while prescribing wind sprints for those under guidance and instruction, extolled the benefits of high levels of physical condition and then headed for the local bar when practice ended, or pointed up the need for team work and cooperation as a means of achieving common goals and then became a dissenting and negative influence in personal and family affairs.

I. John had always been told in junior high school that sport constituted an important medium through which the lessons of sportsmanship and citizenship were taught and broke down racial barriers through actual playing experiences. He came to believe in these values. He felt that there was a high sense of tolerancy of people toward others who were unlike themselves. When John entered high school he played on the football team. On the very first play of his first game, he carried the ball on the kickoff. After being tackled, and in the ensuing pile-up, he was verbally, highly insulted by one of the opponents who used vituperative remarks against John's ethnic background. This initial experience in high school sports left John with a feeling of having to re-evaluate his feelings about the positive social values of sport.

J. A sports coach erased the physical fitness test scores on the final written exam of the athletes in his physical education class in an effort to improve the total grade point average for eligibility purposes. The action was discovered and publicly reported. What decision or alternative actions should be proposed in resolving the situation? Which action can you best support? What reasons can be given for your decision?

K. The student teacher in physical education secured the written final exam prior to the time it was to be given in class and then gave copies to friends who were in the class. The instructor discovered the action after the test had been given. It was then too late to readminister a substitute exam. The instructor contemplated the following steps:

a. Give the student teacher a failing grade.
b. Report the student teacher and recommend dismissal from school.
c. Report the student teacher and recommend a transfer out of the major field.
d. Reprimand the student teacher and offer guidance for the future.
e. Give all failing grades to the friends of the student teacher who received the exam.
f. Complete all grades without the final exam being included.

Reject any of the above alternatives that seem inappropriate, add any of your own, select one or two, and then analyze and compare all appropriate alternatives and choose the best one.

11. The coach instructs the players to hold the opponents through hooking, grasping, or other means which represent techniques contrary to the rules. Should the players follow instructions or speak out against them? Explain the basis for your decision.

Chapter 2

A METHOD OF ETHICAL JUDGMENT
AND PRINCIPLE CONSTRUCTION

$\mathbf{A}$ METHOD of arriving at principles of human conduct is essential in promoting actions toward ends which are considered to be right or good as contrasted with those which may be wrong or bad. How does one construct statements of principles which aid in the formulation of decisions concerning right conduct? There are two words in this question which require definition and understanding prior to an attempt to answer the question.

PRINCIPLE DEFINED

The first word to be clarified is *principle. A principle is a statement of truth which issues from scientific facts or philosophical concepts and theories which, when applied, serves as a guide for actions or decisions concerning the education and/or welfare (right or good) of persons.*

Truth which is based upon the facts of science is not difficult to discover or make meaningful. The fields of applied anatomy, physics, kinesiology, and biomechanics provide ample opportunity for application of scientific fact to the teaching, coaching, and analysis of physical movement. Thus, for example, Newton's *Second Law of Motion* or *Law of Acceleration* applied to human motion states that the rate of change of momentum of a body is proportional to the force, inversely proportional to the mass of the body, and takes place in the direction in which the force acts. This law stated as a principle is universal in its application to the development of efficiency in movement. An understanding of other scientific principles, such as the *Principle of Inertia, Principle of Action and Reaction,* the *Resolution of Forces,* or the influencing factors on the

31

control of the center of gravity, are applied daily by the teacher of physical education and sport. Other principles which issue from work and exercise physiology are indispensible in the development of human efficiency endeavors or in the human physiological training process. The application of principles from motor learning with their substantial base in psychology considerably aids in understanding and facilitating the learning process in physical skill development.

Scientific principles, therefore, may serve as guides for actions by persons toward achieving goals which they consider as good and worthwhile.

Principles which issue from philosophical concepts or ethical theories are not as easy to formulate or apply as precisely as are those which are constructed on the basis of scientific facts. It is often most difficult to secure a consensus of opinion concerning what is right or good in specific circumstances of particular cases of human action. The concept of what is right may differ among individuals based upon diverse backgrounds of growing up, environmental communities, parents, teachers, peer groups, religions, political beliefs, and economic circumstances. People often rely upon a variety of sources for moral guidance, which in turn help to explain their conduct. Among these sources of guidance are custom (regarding as wrong those activities that are contrary to the practices of the group and as right those acts which are in harmony with established practices); statutory law (regulations concerning what must be done and what must not be done with penalties for violations); conscience (an inner faculty or sense of obligation related to moral distinctions that must be obeyed); and religious institutions or a divinely inspired source (the belief in a revelation as a final and absolute truth or moral matter).

How persons develop and apply principles which serve to guide their lives through the decisions they make when such principles issue from a philosophical and ethical context is a complex process. We shall explore a process for accomplishing the task in such a way that it can be applied to questions of ethical decisions in physical education and competitive sports.

The second word in the question to be answered, How does

one construct statements of principles which aid in the formulation of decisions concerning right conduct? is the word *right,* that is, moral rightness as the central concept in ethics. A precise definition of the term *right* is not simple, but the model which we shall establish will attempt to approximate an applicable standard in the context of actions and decisions in our field of study.

The entire field of ethics revolves around the study of right and wrong in human conduct. A search for a definition of the word *right* simply provides at this point a clarification of terms which permits a basis for continuing consideration of the question, How does one construct statements of principles which aid in the formulation of decisions concerning right conduct? The definition of the word *principle* implied that right and good from a moral sense indicates that which promotes good or has value for people in terms of their personal and group welfare.

The basic moral postulate in a democratic society is always centered upon the person in terms of dignity, worth, and respect. The effect of actions on the total personality (intellectual, physical, moral, social, emotional, cultural) is considered in this concept. Any circumstance which contributes positively to this condition is right; any that detracts or denies or hurts the person is wrong. But a judgment as to whether or not an act is right is not simple. Titus and Keeton[38] point out its complexity by inquiring as to whether in judging we should consider the motive a person has in mind (a desire which causes a person to act), the consequences of the act (results that flow from any specific action), or the means used to achieve the end or goal.

CRITERIA FOR DETERMINING RIGHT

Any definition of right decision or right action which attempts to be comprehensive will satisfy the following criteria:

1. The definition must be specific, that is, it must relate specifically to decisions or the actions which result from the decisions rather than to such things as attitudes or beliefs.

2. It must, in contrast to a wrong decision, be involved with voluntary conduct and therefore include the element of choice.
3. The purpose of the action or decision must be for the greatest possible good or, in circumstances where flexibility in judgment is essential, for the least possible harm.
4. It should not be considered as an absolute but rather as the best practical alternative that can be provided under the circumstances — for example, if there are two alternatives, the best is right.
5. It is better than any other practical alternative as determined by intelligently comparing consequences, a process which satisfies conditions of weighing comparative values.
6. It is used to better judge the actions that ordinary reasoning would foresee or anticipate by the largest number, thus envisaging consequences for other people.

As a practical application of the criteria, let us propose a decision made by a teacher of physical education under circumstances involving a dress code or uniform clothing for all students enrolled in classes.

Should all students be required to wear a standard uniform during institutional classes in physical education? Support for a standard uniform argues that discrimination is eliminated, that is, discrepancies between types of dress that can be afforded by the more affluent and the type worn by the economically disadvantaged are diminished; the uniform provides a leveling of social and economic distinctions; quality control of dress factors is afforded; supervision of cleanliness factors are more readily available and easier to administer; and the safety of students is governed by the standardization of uniform specifications rather than permitting a wide variation of differences which may incur possible accident incidents.

On the other hand, students should not be forced into an economic situation which they are not capable of meeting in the event of costs of the uniform; the freedom of expression concerning dress is an individual factor within limits of safety specifications; hygiene inspection may be conducted irrespective of dress quality or styles; and a dress code is irrelevant to achieving performance objectives in courses of instruction.

Alternative decisions related to right action might range from the absolute rule that all students must conform to standard uniform specifications to permitting complete freedom of expression in dress styles. Neither of these actions or decisions, however, might satisfy the criteria that has been established for the definition of right. There are alternative or intermediate type decisions that lie between the two extremes indicated. A review of the consequences or conditions that might result in terms of the purposes of the uniform code or the freedom of dress provision may lead to the adoption of the standard uniform, but with the flexibility that the uniform would be of reasonable or minimum cost and that students who could not afford to purchase it would be provided the uniform from a pool of collected uniforms or from other sources available for this purpose.

The application of the criteria for judging right decisions reveals a satisfaction of the conditions established in the criteria and a compliance with the definition of principle in terms of its implication for right and good for a moral sense as applied to promoting value for people in terms of the personal welfare.

Mitchell,[22] after having analyzed definitions of the term *right* proposed by modern philosophical theorists, presents a definition which is precise and meets the indicated criteria. With some modification, right related to conduct may be defined as "to be right is to carry out the chosen alternative, which, insofar as consequences can be foreseen, will leave the total situation better than would any other action that one could have taken in terms of the most intrinsic good or the least intrinsic evil for persons" (p. 172).

Thus, the list of criteria for right is complete: it claims universality; it recognizes action as voluntary; it stresses practicality; it suggests the use of foresight; it includes the total situation and thus moral distribution; it makes right a comparative matter; it provides for flexibility in judgment; it includes the comparison of consequences; and it demonstrates compassion for people.

The next step, after having clarified the words *principle* and *right,* is to proceed with seeking an answer to the question, How does one construct statements of principles which aid in the formulation of decisions concerning right conduct? The precise answer to this question is through the development of a method or systematic model which will direct thinking along lines to provide for logic in procedure, comprehensiveness in treatment, and validation of findings or statements of principle.

NEED FOR A METHOD

Established principles, customs, traditions, conscience, law, and religion are often not sufficient in themselves to assist one in arriving at decisions or taking actions in an ethical context. "No past decision nor old principle," stated Dewey,[6] "can ever be wholly relied upon to justify a course of action" (pp. 174-175). Often principles, standards, and customs conflict with each other. Values do change, and the older ways of doing things and of weighing alternatives are not always applicable to newer situations. The complexity of some situations makes it impossible to follow a rule-of-thumb statement related to a fixed pattern of behavior. This does not mean to imply that established cases of conduct, legal history, judicial decisions, the sciences, or a system of moral thought developed through the centuries of time are to be put aside. It simply indicates that an explicit method to guide thinking toward the formulation of an ethical judgment concerning right conduct is better when choices are (1) guided by a body of knowledge controlled so as to provide foresight or probable consequences with possible adjustments according to changing circumstances, (2) tested as to validity, and (3) weighted according to value outcomes for people and their educational and personal welfare.

An example of the complexity of a situation in physical education and sport which would seem to require the application of an explicit method, fulfilling the conditions indicated in the foregoing paragraph to achieve solutions to its problems, is that expressed by the President's Commission on Olympic Sports. A review of the procedures applied by the President's

Commission reveals that, consciously or not, such conditions were met.*

The Commission's final report to be made to the President of the United States after a comprehensive collection of information included such substantive items as

1. An expansion and restructuring of amateur sports in the United States, including a revised concept of amateurism.
2. A restructured/reconstituted United States Olympic Committee.
3. The establishment of a *higher sports authority* to settle franchise disputes, hear complaints, preserve human rights in sports, provide for the representation of the United States in international sports, and eliminate power struggles among sport organizations and individuals.
4. The establishment of a federal agency to coordinate and stimulate research in athletics.
5. An expansion of a comprehensive program of athletics for women.
6. A strengthened *Bill of Rights* for athletes to assure their fundamental rights.

Underlying all deliberations of the President's Commission was the recognition of the primary responsibility of organizations and institutions which administer sport to possess a basic concern for the individual participant. Such a concern clearly focused the substance of the deliberations on the ethical nature of the immense dilemma confronting amateur sport in this country.

Decisions are more apt to be right when subjected to disciplined thinking through the application of elements of a method whose supporting theories and data revolve around a central core of criteria concerning what is right. Judgments in ethical matters require the same diligent application of method

*Reference should be made to the series of *Commission News* published by the President's Commission on Olympic Sports, 2025 M. Street, N.W., Suite 3002, Washington, D.C., Gerald B. Zornow, Chairman, Beverly L. Dodd, Communications Department, 1976.

as do judgments in the biological and natural sciences. In fact, the ethical study experience in the absence of a method which is well-structured and tested, consciously adopted, and conscientiously followed cannot qualify as one which can be justified on a sound or scientific basis.

Too often people utilize the so-called Monday-morning-quarterback style of thinking when rendering opinions by (1) failing to secure the facts, (2) failing to apply reflective thought, (3) compensating for their judgments through preformed prejudices and biases, (4) becoming resentful or violent under repressive thoughts, (5) resorting to a general cover-all theory, or (5) adopting some widely expressed statement as truth without subjecting it to a tested method of evaluation.

Consider, for example, the statement, "Winning is not the most important thing, it is the only thing." This statement has received widespread acceptance and application among, of all people, many in the environment of our educational institutions whose avowed purposes, on close examination, do not acknowledge such a purpose. Yet, the evaluation of such a statement when made and applied within the context of education and in light of our already formulated definition of a principle and the criteria for right would seem to require considerable treatment. An individual or a group might provide considerable thought and time to the analysis of this statement. But, unless they are guided by a method or a systematic model which can logically structure thinking, they may not provide the statement with comprehension in treatment, substantive and validated support for conclusions, nor well-formulated statements of principles for guidance.

There is a good basis for understanding a need for a method for ethical judgment and for construction of principles for future direction in ethical actions. A review of the codes within law, religion, and custom, as well as the substantive academic disciplines, demonstrates the arrangement of fundamental concepts and principles into a coherent, logical structure. Such a structure provides a context which serves as a framework of reference within which one may seek guidance for logical thinking.

The important point to note is that it *is* possible for a method to be used in arriving at ethical judgments which permit even tentative hypotheses to fit into the structure of a method and be tested for validity. We shall attempt to demonstrate this on the section on validation of method. While a partially empirical science (one based on practical experience and observation without reference to scientific principles) cannot be entirely deductive (reasoning from a known principle to an unknown), its assumptions taken as self-evident (postulate) may be made explicit and systematic.

BASIC ELEMENTS OF A METHOD

One cannot expect to develop a statement of principle out of a vacuum. Theories related to ethical behavior, just as theories which have their basis in science, require (1) a body of substantive and dependable data upon which to refer for support and (2) a set of intelligible working hypotheses. As already explained in Chapter 1, the scientific method applied to physical theories is exact and highly directive for thinking. The scientist asks, How can the philosophers arrive at precise, valid judgments concerning right and wrong conduct of human beings through the means of reflective thought and without the means of controlling an extensive set of variables existing within human nature?

It is possible to suggest a systematic model to direct thinking in a positive and logical manner so as to derive answers, even tentatively, to the questions, Why should one act this way and not otherwise? Why is this right and that wrong? Hill[11] indicates a simple model by pointing out that all one would find necessary would be to determine the probable consequences of each alternative course of action and then make a comparative evaluation of these sets of consequences. The set that proves to have the most total value over disvalue for all would be the one whose causative act would be right. But situations involving ethical decisions may not be limited as to permit so simple a solution.

Method Defined

A definition of method will assist one to better grasp the essential elements which comprise a method. A simple definition often referred to is that which denotes any procedure which applies some rational order or systematic pattern. A more complete definition would be that *a method is a structured, controlled, procedural, systematic pattern which permits a manipulation of responses and is capable of reproducing a logical order of such responses; it permits a methodic and logical application of endeavors into the pursuit of predetermined or generally recognizable purposes.* While there are different types of methods which can be applied under varying circumstances, the type of method with which we are concerned is that which demands rationality and is capable of questioning, criticizing, and testing.

From the information which has been presented up to this point we might, by way of summary, indicate that the basic elements contained in a method of ethical judgment and logical reasoning are the following:

1. A structured procedure for disciplined thinking within a framework which is dialectic and analytical in nature.
2. A provision for the application of supporting theories and data, together with a method of validating such support.
3. A thoughtful consideration of all objectives, facts, and alternatives that can be made available.
4. A set of established criteria upon which judgment may be made at those critical points where conflicts in discussions or reasoning are apt to occur. (An example might be in instances where there are questions as to whether or not an action or decision is right.)
5. A means of developing tentative hypotheses, together with their testing and verification.
6. An insistence on high objectivity in treatment from investigators of vested interests or personalities or of the moral postulations of individuals and groups.
7. A controlled, ordered, and purposeful means for testing the ends or goals achieved.

REFLECTIVE THINKING

When attempting to state a general principle, standard, or hypothesis which may direct or justify a decision related to conduct, one engages in systematic reflective thinking on ethical theory. Ethical theory is no more than asking, What is the right or best thing to do? In decisions involving moral perplexity, in doubt as to what is right or wrong, one attempts to find the way out by weighing all the facts involved by bringing to bear all of the elements which comprise a base of morals. One engages in reflective thought in searching for a reasonable standard or principle by which to decide where the right really lies.

Athletes may possess an intense desire to strive to their utmost in order to help the team to win. Many possess a strong loyalty and attachment to the team, and at the moment, winning is the most important force in their lives. But when shown how the application of certain techniques, which decidedly take advantage of their competitors in a manner contrary to the spirit of the rules of the game (but not expressly included in the rules), can assist the team to win, athletes are confronted with moral conflict. Many do not, by their nature, acquiesce in unsportsmanlike behavior. They experience a conflict between the incompatible values presented to them. They are forced to reflect in order to come to a decision.

Benefits of Reflective Thinking

Reflection on the issues can help to make a more intelligent personal decision as to what to do, but the decision must still be made as it does in every case of ethical perplexity. Reflection can assist to clarify the problem by seeing it in a larger context than simply the immediate situation; it can point out alternative ways of dealing with the situation in terms of differing consequences resulting from each; and it can render personal thinking more systematic and enlightened and possibly provide a greater consistency in judgment.

From the standpoint of aiding one to formulate a standard as to what should or ought to be done, reflection permits crystal-lizing one's thoughts to a point of establishing, even though tentatively, a value judgment concerning one's behavior in the context of one's own life.

Several incidents may be cited wherein the sports performer, prospective teacher, or coach may have sufficient time to reflect prior to arriving at a decision concerning conduct and conse-quences.

The sports performer must reach a decision on whether or not to take amphetamines prior to the conference track and field championships as a questionable means of enhancing performance and capturing the championship title for the final athletic performance or his or her college athletic career.

The physical education student who abhors corporal punish-ment (paddling) when used as a corrective measure for rule infractions in physical education must decide whether or not to request a change in a student teaching assignment to another high school, administer the corporal punishment when re-quested, or exert personal effort to change the situation.

The assistant coach who also teaches a physical fitness class is confronted with a decision whether or not to change the final grades so as to improve the grade point average and academic eligibility status of the coach's athletes who are enrolled in the class.

A distinction is made between customary morality and reflec-tive morality. The former consists of a largely uncritical adop-tion and use of inherited ways of judging conduct and orienting one's way of life. The primary purpose of reflective morality as related to a philosophical system of ethics is to give some reasoned account for one's choices of standards.

There has been in this day a tendency to minimize the need for reflective thinking in moral issues. Some say that everyone has an idea of what works for him or her and what does not, a process that has to do with intuition and not intellectual anal-ysis. Hill[11] points out that in the vast majority of instances in which voluntary choices must be made no serious difficulty is encountered in doing the right thing. Most persons act in ac-cordance with the prevailing mores and their own consciences with the confidence that the decisions or actions are right. In fact, in such cases, taking time to debate within oneself may lead to fear of making ethical mistakes and dread of frustration. At the same time, one is not to become too complacent or gloss over some decisions simply because the manner of acting or deciding can be based on custom, traditions, the standards of one's profession, or a rationalizing conscience. One needs to periodically review his or her own ethical principles and re-examine his or her usual patterns of thought to prevent some social or personal injustices that can result.

There are innumerable instances in physical education and in the competitive sport experience where human action toward others is performed in the absence of reflective thinking. Often, there is no time for reflective thought. Consider these examples: The unintentional infliction of injury upon an opponent in the heat of competition in executing a maneuver to assist a play or to stop the contest; the almost automatic response to helping a teammate in difficulty; or providing the opportunity to another to score the winning goal or points when that opportunity is afforded.

Reflective thinking often occurs after the performance when one is away from the scene of action, usually when there exists doubt as to whether the action was right or wrong. One might then reflect upon the consequences of an act already performed. In the instance of an intentional foul committed in order to officially stop the contest, resulting in an injury to the opponent, one might say, "I wouldn't do it if I had the chance again." Dewey[6] indicates that moral theory cannot emerge whenever there is a positive belief as to what is right or wrong, for then there is no cause for reflection. It is only when persons experience a conflict of good ends and rules of right and wrong or incompatible courses of action that ethical theory emerges and reflective thought becomes an essential ingredient in the process.

Relationships Between Conduct in Sports and Life

One of the most fertile fields for reflective thinking for students of physical education and sport is in the development of relationships between behavior or action in the physical activity environment and in that of life generally. For example, the question is often raised, How much assurance is there that the lessons of good sportsmanship or good citizenship learned in the competitive sports experience will carry over or transfer to the ordinary life situations in the home and community? The rules of the game direct human action along lines which are consistent with those expected of good citizenship in a democratic society. The infraction of the rules of the game resulting in penalties against the individual and the team is direct evidence of the need to adhere to such rules, a situation highly related to action in life generally.

The development of discerned relationships between sports experiences and life situations is not apt to automatically occur. What may be needed under well-planned guidance is the opportunity and the means to engage in reflective thinking that asks, Why should I act thus and not otherwise in situations whose outcomes are the same or similar? If it is right for me to show consideration to my teammates by contributing to produce successful performances for both the individual and the team, why in similar instances should I not show consideration to my brother, sister, parent, and neighbor in assisting them to meet responsibilities and burdens which are common to all?

A SYSTEMATIC METHOD OF PRINCIPLE CONSTRUCTION

Eight steps are proposed as a guide to direct thinking along lines which optimally lead to judgment formulation regarding the right decision or action in ethical conduct. The final outcome should result in the structure of statements of principles which can be accepted as sound and acceptable in accordance with the established conditions and in the context of the ethical criteria presented. These steps are as follows:

1. Create a condition of open-mindedness — rejection of

preformed biases or narrow-mindedness.
2. Collect and consider all facts in the total situation.
3. Develop tentative hypotheses (alternatives) in terms of what ought to be the decision or action.
4. Test the hypotheses (alternatives) for validity in terms of what is right. Reject the unacceptable alternatives.
5. Determine probable consequences of the hypotheses (alternatives) selected.
6. Make a comparative evaluation of the probable consequences from each of the selected alternative courses of action.
7. Select the alternative that proves most valid and whose consequences lead to the better or best courses of action in terms of right.
8. Reinforce the choice of alternative.

The analysis of alternatives in terms of testing for validity, comparing consequences, and decisively choosing the best alternative (decision making) are the central figures of the ethical method.

A METHOD OF ETHICAL JUDGMENT

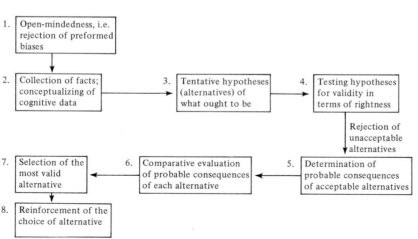

Figure 3.

Step One — Open-mindedness

The first step insists that one must be open-minded, that is, one's mind must be receptive to all views that are to be presented in any moral deliberative process. One must reject bias or narrow-mindedness which attempts to rationalize and seek support for doing what he or she has already decided to do. One cannot, for example, determine the quality of a student's intellectual, physical, moral, or social abilities simply by judging the student's appearance, color, size, religious or political views, or economic status. Teachers and coaches may often make judgments on the character, social, and performance qualities of students on a first appearance basis.

Sound moral deliberation requires a preliminary preparation of mind upon which impartiality is accorded; in a framework of open-mindedness, benevolence to humankind and understanding of one's fellow is as to accord fairness and justice and the value potentiality of all. To think in terms of absolutes often stifles discussion and prevents the consideration of possible alternative courses of action in light of the values to which they may lead. There are values which must be weighed in terms of the circumstances which exist within a specific situation and therefore should not be looked upon as absolute and sacred to be preserved at any cost. Where there are no options, there are no choices and therefore no problems. The most prominent ethical problems in our society are those in which the values are questioned.

Step Two — Collection of Facts

The second step requires a full collection and consideration of the facts in the total situation. The facts will assist in locating and defining difficulties and conflicts. Why is this a problem? Is there a conflict in rules, policies, principles? Or is there a clash of views relative to the need for changing an existing rule? Or are there conflicting interests that must be reconciled or reshaped? Questioning of this kind represents a commonly recognized procedure in administrative processes where decisions must be made relative to not only outcomes for people but also other facets of program progress. Since ethical deliberations are concerned with human beings, it is especially important that all possible facts be brought together and placed into a position where they can be clearly viewed or focused.

The collection of facts in the field of ethics is not as precise as in other fields because we can never achieve a degree of certainty as high as, for example, in the fields of mathematics or physical sciences. The probability or our conclusions vary, therefore, with the complexity of the situation. Without a comprehensive collection and consideration of the facts with their accurate description, ethical deliberations and decisions may be misled. Any intentional omission or deliberate misdirection at this point represents a moral weakness in itself.

An example of the application of this second step could include the case of the violation of training rules established by the athletic coach with punitive measures against violators, yet involving some nonviolators among the accused. Prior to decisions or actions it would be extremely important to secure the facts in the case. Just who were involved and under what circumstances? Was there a consciousness of what was being done? Was there an attempt to alert violators of the accepted standard of conduct prior to the act? Was there an awareness of the consequences?

Stahl[37] indicates that the collection of all data assists one to better identify a specific ethical issue and the moral substance involved in a dilemma and achieve a better understanding of it. The process permits a *focus of moralization* which forces one to view possible conflicting moral-related issues and gain better perspective. It also adds to the need for data, the importance of conceptualizing the data so as to consider the situation as another person might understand and feel the situation. Thus, Stahl goes beyond the mere collection of facts by placing importance on comprehending cognitive information by which one can develop an awareness of another person about whom judgment is to be made so that one can be more receptive and sensitive to another's feelings, needs, and perspectives.

Step Three — Tentative Hypotheses

The third step is to develop tentative hypotheses in terms of what ought to be the decision or action in the particular situation or in a phase of the total situation. After having achieved a state of open-mindedness, with the rejection of bias, and a frame of mind suited to ethical deliberation, having brought all existing facts into clear focus, one must establish possible courses of action that would seem most reasonable. It is at this stage of the deliberative process that one initially engages in reflective thinking, which has already been described. Out of this process may issue several lines of action or alternatives that may qualify to meet the criteria of right and good, in whole or in part.

The question that arises is, How does one construct a hypothesis even of a tentative nature? The process is a highly intellectual one which is conditioned by the factors of (1) the availability of time to reflect, (2) the possession of all of the facts involved in the circumstances, and (3) a consciousness of criteria that has previously been established to judge the rightness and goodness of human action and decision. A hypothesis is simply a statement or proposition that is tentatively assumed so as to draw out its logical or empirical meanings and consequences against the facts that have been collected. It represents a statement that is to be either proved or disproved by comparing it with the facts.

In this sense, the student who engages in the ethical study experience applies a method for arriving at the truth concerning what is right or wrong. The reference to the criteria of right within the context of particular circumstances for guidance in developing hypotheses with due accord to the factual material available follows the pattern of method used in the natural and physical sciences. The initial step in the process is the establishment of hypotheses or tentative solutions to a problem.

An illustration of the application of step three of the method to a practical situation in sport might be made by raising the question, After having collected all of the facts, what possible alternative actions could be considered by the coach in the previously cited case of the violation of training rules by members of the sport team?

One might also establish a sample hypothesis in evaluating the statement, "Winning is not the most important thing, it is the only thing," as the statement is directly applied to the program of sports in schools and colleges. After having brought all of the existing facts into clear focus, and after having considered all of the educational implications of the statement, one might formulate the following hypothesis:

> Our educational institutions and their programs (athletics) should be considered as a means of educating students and not as an end in themselves.

Thus, the hypothesis is suggested by recognizing certain common elements among others which are regarded as good and right within the primary purposes of educational institutions and as implied in the definition of a basic principal, which in a democratic society is difficult to refute.

Commonly heard refutations to the hypothesis statement are as follows:

> If we don't win, I'll be out of a job and face a threat to my security. And me and mine come first.

or

> In a free enterprise system that recognizes resourcefulness, initiative, and industriousness, the ones who get to the top are those who win, not the losers. If you want to get to the top, winning is the only thing.

Step Four — Testing Hypotheses for Validity

The fourth step consists of testing the hypotheses for their validity in terms of what is right.

A recognition of the criteria that aids in judging right action is essential. One is thus able to single out two or three lines of action indicated in statements of hypotheses that are likely to lead in the direction of right decision and avoid wrong and bad value judgments.

While step three included the need for a consciousness of the criteria for judging rightness, it is at this point in step four that the tentative hypotheses must be tested for their reasonableness and acceptability. A brief review of the criteria for judging the degree of which an act may be right follows:

a. It must relate specifically to the resulting decisions or actions and not to beliefs or attitudes, etc.
b. It must be involved with voluntary conduct and include the element of choice.
c. It must be for the greatest possible good or least possible harm.
d. It must not be an absolute but represent the best possible alternative under the circumstances.
e. It must be better than any other practical alternative by comparing consequences or weighing comparative values.
f. It must consider consequences for other or all people by anticipating or foreseeing results on the largest numbers.

Thus, as one tests each statement of hypothesis against the criteria, some questions to be asked are, Does it provide the best possible alternative under the circumstances? Does it, compared with other judgment statements, provide for a choice of action so as to establish a basis for comparative values? Does it provide the greatest possible good or the least possible harm in terms of consequences that are likely to result? Does it represent a standard which a person of ordinary practical reason could anticipate, that is, be able to foresee rightness of action based upon the knowledge available? Does it provide for some flexibility in terms of the possibilities of adjustments or reasonable compromises to be made at a future date, without at the same time having to sacrifice the criterion or criteria or having to confront unavailable necessities?

It is to be noted that this step, consisting of testing hypotheses related to right and wrong action or decision, provides a freedom of choice, even though it may be somewhat limited. This approach may conflict with other approaches in the application of ethical theories with which we shall deal later. It does offer a means of arriving at the better or best of alternative decisions whose alternatives are now to be considered.

Step Five — Determination of Consequences

The fifth step is to determine probable consequences of the hypotheses (alternatives) selected. Let us return to the rather simple illustration of the athletic coach who established a rule forbidding smoking during the training and playing season of the sport under the threat of expulsion of violators of the rule.

The consequences of such an absolute rule could be disastrous to the individual student, to the team, and to the school in comparison to other alternative measures that might have been established which would have still led to the results desired by the coach, i.e. the adherence to the rules of training. A possible alternative could consist of the establishment of guidelines for training behavior which, if violated, would place the coach into a position to provide guidance and education as a function of coaching and teaching. The consequences of such action would be considerably different than those resulting from the application of absolute rules. Another alternative of an intermediate nature could consist of disciplinary action of a short-term nature such as having to "sit out" the next scheduled game. The consequences of this action in terms of ethical implications might be different than the two previous options mentioned. There may be other alternative courses of action, all of which may present varied consequences.

The central questions asked in this step are, What will be the results of possible courses of action that might be taken? What values will be achieved in terms of their educational implications on the welfare of the individual(s) and the group(s) (team, school, community) by the options which are available? It is to be noted that the ethical dimensions of consequences focus on not merely the material or manifestations of winning or losing, but rather on the indication of the consequences from a right or wrong or moral view. This is an often overlooked concept of decision makers. Consequences of actions which involve moral implications should, therefore, indicate ethical values.

The example related to violation of training rules is rather provincial in nature. While principles may have direct meanings for those most intimately involved, that is, those who are most closely associated with the decision-making incident, a person must enlarge one's perspectives to discern the relationships of the principle to a broader circle of humans and human actions. A question that might well be asked is, What are the moral effects of my proposed courses of action upon the moral standards of my community, state, and nation, and ultimately upon the lives of all humankind?

Step Six — Comparative Evaluation of Consequences

The sixth step involves the making of a comparative evaluation of the probable consequences from each of the alternative courses of action. This step may be further explained by indicating that one must list or look at each proposed course of action and determine those outcomes in terms of ethical values that are apt to result from each action or decision. These values will be those which are more reasonable and good in the sense of their yielding outcomes or consequences which are worthy for the sake of the individual(s) involved and for others in their experiential sense. Hill[11] suggests that the values to be considered be intrinsic in nature, that is, that they be considered principally on the basis of their goodness in themselves to produce intrinsically good experiences. What, for example, will be the consequences of the three alternative decisions which the coach might make in the case of training violations? To what extent do the consequences of each decision have on the individuals, the team, the school, and the community? What will be the actual moral effect on the individuals, not only in terms of the present but for the remainder of their lives?

Since this step is concerned with a process of comparative evaluation, it implies that the concern is also with one of degree. To what degree do each of the consequences of each course of action or decision have on the raising or lowering of ethical standards, in promoting better or worse social attitudes, in establishing better or poorer personal habits of conduct, and in contributing to the formation of what is generally called character, good or bad?

Kant[15], who placed unconditional value in character, offered two interesting facets of his moral law which have bearing on this deliberative process. One of these would increase the degree of the consequences of a possible course of action by indicating that everyone act on the rule universally.

Kant's *Moral Law* or *The Categorical Imperative* stated, "Act on the maxim (or rule) and that maxim only, which you could will to become by your act a universal law of nature." Suppose one was to invoke this formal, universal, and absolute law in the situation on athletic training previously presented. The consequences would be multiplied many times, and the tendency of such consequences, if the rule was to be applied in an absolute way and to all such situations, would be clear to see. Thus an athlete who revolts against rules of training and identifies a conflict between personal freedoms and the disciplinary rule of coaches may establish an implicit rule, such as to break the rules of training if they are inconvenient and uncomfortable. The athlete must then ask, "Suppose all athletes or members of the team break the rules of training whenever they wish; what would be the result?"

One may experience considerable difficulty in projecting and evaluating comparative sequences of expected outcomes and without excessive consideration of details. There often exists instances where the evaluator lacks a substantial enough background of experience in such matters and would find difficulty in noting the full ramifications of a probable set of consequences. The ethical study experience can be helpful in securing practice in mastery of the technique. One becomes more able to screen out the seemingly wrong or bad or evil consequences compared to the right or good, while indicating consequences which possess the greatest amount of good.

Although it has been previously indicated that reference to old principle, custom, tradition, conscience, law, or religion are often not sufficient in themselves in the decision-making process, in an ethical context one may find considerable assistance in reviews of established moral theory and insight. Discussion with others such as afforded in the classroom environment or among experienced and respected persons may assist in providing an orientation to the comparative evaluative process. In this way, one may move closer to a course of action whose consequences will demonstrate a maximum good, comparatively, for all or for most people involved and be as near right, comparatively, as thoughtful and objective analysis may lead.

Step Seven — Choice of Alternative (Decision)

The seventh step consists of the selection of the alternative that proves most valid and whose consequences lead to the better, right, and good. Having earlier tested the alternatives (hypotheses) for validity through their subjection to the criteria of right, thus avoiding wrong or bad value judgments, and having projected and comparatively evaluated the probable consequences of the remaining alternatives, we are now ready to perform a summary judgment. Having placed the remaining alternatives into a position for selection, one may ask, On what basis can a final selection be made?

It is important at this point to review the definition of a principle, which, in the final analysis, is our prime interest in establishing a method for ethical guidance and direction. We are interested in determining the truth or moral right which may serve to guide decisions or actions involving the education and/or welfare of persons. We look upon what is right as a means to all else that is good. If the choice of the alternative which, insofar as the consequences are foreseeable, will leave the situation as a whole better than would any other, the action or decision is right. Our judgment is to be based upon the consequences of the action in terms of the welfare of everyone involved with due regard to the universality of its application to all living organisms. This concept implies that we do not need to be concerned with the elements of motives, intentions, or character among others. These will be accounted for in due course if the decision maker is objectively right.

The question before us is, How might one make the selection of the alternative which is most valid and whose consequences lead to the better right and good? Isn't it enough that a rough estimate of consequences and their values will be sufficient to enable one to make a final selection of the proper alternative? However, one might also ask, Can there be more assurance that a selection is objectively right than simply the calculations of probable consequences of alternative decisions or courses of actions?

There are some who possess sufficient faith to think that with the alternatives narrowed to those which meet the criteria of right and whose consequences are most reasonable, the ultimate and final judgment or decision based on moral integrity will virtually be properly judged even in a subjective manner, that the probability of the best objective judgment of the correct selection will most certainly be present, and that in terms of the ultimate higher right, the final judgment will be within proximity. This type of thinking deserves consideration because it is projected upon the experiences of having to treat human affairs with its difficulty in controlling human variables. To fall short of perfectionism in judging the priority of values and the probable consequences of human actions is completely human.

The selection of the proper alternative or decision could end in a rather simple manner by stating that the set of consequences which contains the greatest balance of intrinsic value, or the least of evil, and most highly meets the criteria for good indicates that the alternative is right in the circumstances.[11] A better sense of direction, however, is needed if one is to attempt to arrange fundamental concepts and principles as a coherent logical structure.

The ranking of values is primarily the task of the ethical study experience. That is to say, the whole field of values comes under the scope of moral philosophy. When one judges the ranking of values, he or she ranks things in order of better or worse. The selection of alternatives on the basis of their value rank is actually a task of making comparisons or of pairing. If we could reduce qualitative differences to some common measure, such as standard weights or dollars and cents, the comparison and selection of alternatives would be much easier. But again, preciseness in the weighing of human values may not always be desirable, but rather, because of comparative qualitative factors, flexibility in forming judgments may be preferred.

The process of making comparisons and of pairing comparable value characteristics brings us very closely into the field of logic. For example, the comparative nature of valuation suggests a scale of values. If A is better than the nonexistence of A, then A is good. If B is better than A, and C is better than B, we have ranked these elements of good in a scale. There might also be a scale of bad things and bad practices. If the nonexistence of M is better than its existence, then M is bad. If N is worse than M, and O is worse than N, and P is worse than O, we have a scale of badness. Thus, we can have a scale of values arranged in serial order above and below a dividing line between good and bad with the line consisting of those elements that are indifferent.[21]

It would seem that, in practice, the comparison of values related to alternative choices of conduct depends, to a large degree, on the possibility of analyzing factors that can be paired. If two or more alternatives have components which are the same or are common to both, it is logical that these components should be cancelled out. Or, if a number of factors within the alternatives are of approximately equal value and can thus be paired, these also can be cancelled. As a result of such a process, decisions can be made on the basis of the remaining points of difference. The differences must then be ranked in accordance with the best knowledge and judgment of the judge.

One may feel that this procedure lends itself to judgments which are absolute and detracts from a need for flexibility, a characteristic which is of extreme importance in dealing with human values. The criticism could be entirely correct, except that at this point one enters into a remaining procedure — that of performing a summary judgment concerned with the relationships between all values in all remaining alternatives. This process consists of standing off and viewing possible interrelated values existing in a reciprocal relationship. It involves the possible further adjustments or modifications of values in the total matrix of values so as to harmonize them and bring them into position to better contribute to the total good in accordance to one's higher sense of value judgments.

Step Eight — Reinforcement of Choice (Decision)

The eighth and final step consists of the reinforcement of the decision or choice of hypotheses. This step requires the strengthening or substantiating of the choice of judgment. It requires answers to the questions, On what grounds is my judgment correct? What evidence is there that my judgment is a substantial one? To what sources might I refer to further strengthen the judgment preference? What reasons can be given to further support the moral judgment?

These are somewhat different questions from those related to whether any action or decision is right. Having applied the criteria for rightness to our hypotheses, and having made a judgment on the basis of the rightness criteria, we must now enter into the reinforcement of the value judgment. Having accepted, for example, a moral judgment based on the criteria of rightness, such as

> Women in sport should (ought to) be accorded the same
> rights, privileges, and conditions for participation as men,

we must now proceed to reinforce the statement. Is the statement in harmony with self-evident principles or contrary to them? Is it conducive to the development of human personality as recognized in the basic beliefs of a democratic society, or is it antagonistic toward them? Does the statement, in its implications, violate or enhance principles of good health or physiological and psychological functions? Is it contrary to the principles of social justice to humankind, or is it supported by such truths?

The grounds for support of ethical judgments are distinctly philosophical ones. However, an effort to discover the answers to such questions will carry us beyond the methods of philosophy and into other fields of knowledge, such as the basic and applied sciences of physiology of work and exercise, psychology, motor learning, sociology, and anthropology. Other avenues of inquiry may cause ventures into theology and religion relative to human justice, to law for legal justification, to deductive logic for self-evident principles. It is during this process of seeking reinforcement of ethical decisions or choices that we discover the relationship between ethics and the sciences, both social and natural, as well as other sources of data.

Dewey and Tufts[5] suggest four sources of data in support of moral theory and working hypotheses. These are as follows:

1. Established codes of conduct. All professions possess codes which serve as guides for professional and personal conduct or what is proper and fair in human relations. (An illustration of such codes is provided in Chapter 6.)
2. Legal history, judicial decisions, and legislative activity. These have evolved in long experimentation in working out directions for human beings in their conduct. All great human institutions (family, government, education, etc.) contain records of modes of human conduct and the consequences of choice of conduct. Biographies of the great moral teachers also represent sources of such data.
3. Biological, natural, and social sciences. An example of the relationship between personal and national health and moral interests and responsibilities with the moral order may be substantiated from this source of data.
4. A system of moral thought including theoretical methods and conclusions which have characterized European and Asiatic history and doctrines for over 2000 years. Each system of moral thought presents a point of view from which present facts may be looked at and studied.

THE VALIDATION OF METHOD

How rational or at least how reasonable is the method? The place to look for rationality of method is in the validation of the reasoning behind it. As in the methods of science, theories must be subjected to test and confirmation and respond to substantiation or, in a sense, to validation. The purpose of testing a method as to its validity is to determine whether or not the process of formulating standards or principles of ethical conduct are merely speculation or are valid. Otherwise, the process of thinking, discussion, and deduction may become speculative, or in the more common description, "bull-throwing."

A verifiable set of criteria placed into a logical order in a method helps to determine whether or not cognitively significant statements are capable of validation. The method suggested in the text provides for such criteria. The critera of right and the steps which lead to logical analysis permit the determination of judgments to be valid, or most valid, and other judgments as not acceptable.

Ross[31] provides a view worth examination:

> Methods of science are but one kind of method; other methods have their own means of validation and their own kinds of tests. I suggest, however, that unless there is a method — that is, control, order, purpose — there cannot be validation. An action becomes capable of validation only within an order with determinable goals and ends. It is either valid because it is good for some purpose or insofar as it satisfies implicit or explicit criteria of appraisal. Validation cannot exist without an ordered sense of method. It is legitimate to ask "how?" And the sense of this question is "How did you do it? Can you do it again?" — implying the existence of a method. If there is no answer available to these questions, tests for validity are empty. (p. 76)

Ross's quotation indicates that it is not enough to reply to the question as to the derivation of a judgment in terms of "because I feel that way," or "that's the way it is," and walk away from it. Those types of replies are unintelligible and have no relation to validity. One might achieve positive results through the method of trial and error, but the method is a haphazard one, and a precarious one at best, when applied to judgments affecting education and the welfare of people.

Testing for Validity

Validation depends on the existence of a means for testing actions — whether or not the means applied meets particular standards. The tests that are used are presented in the form of questions related to the very nature of the goals sought and reside in the context of the definition of method as presented here.

Consider, for example, the judgments of the Executive Secretary of the National Federation of State High School Associations relative to the very critical problem of control of the conduct of players in high school athletic contests.[7] These judgments were projected following increased incidents of fighting during or following high school sport events which involved, as well as players, fans other than students.

1. The head of the school and the director of athletics must impress upon the coach that fighting by players will not be tolerated under any condition. Coaches must support the premise that an athletic contest is an educational experience, and as such, fighting is not part of it.

2. Coaches must accept that one of their principle obligations is to control the members of their squads. If a coach is unable to discharge this responsibility, he or she needs to be replaced.

3. Coaches must make certain that players representing their schools do not intimidate or attempt to intimidate opponents or officials. Some coaches consider intimidation as an aspect of "psyching up" for a contest. This attitude is intolerable. Intimidation is the first step toward a situation which eventually becomes uncontrollable.

4. Athletic directors must make certain they engage and then aggressively support only those officials who administer the game according to the letter and spirit of the rules. In virtually every situation which gets out of control, the officials contribute to it by not administering the rules properly, that is, by failing to call violations and fouls consistently and promptly.

5. Those who are responsible for hiring athletic coaches must engage only coaches who have the proper athletic philosophy for interscholastic competition, and they must know what the philosophy of the coach is before employment. Then they must see to it that the philosophy is followed implicitly.

The subjection of these judgments to the criteria provided in the method proposed in this text permits one to test the validity of the judgments. What are the *facts* in the total situation that precipitated such judgments? What are the underlying purposes of each of these judgments in terms of their effects upon the welfare of the players, the students, the school and community, and on the future of sport in the high schools? What are the outcomes of weighing each of these judgments against the criterion of what is right? What might be the consequences of these judgments or of different or no judgments?

The Interrogative Method

The act of asking questions (interrogative method) permits a person to test what one does or wants to do. It is upon this procedure that one constructs a rationality for one's actions or decisions — providing, of course, that there are provisions for validation. Interrogative methods are essential to assure that principles are being applied rather than blind habits. Acting rightly implies an interrogative method with rules of validation. Without appraisal, one can only act routinely or blindly. *Without means of validation, one's actions are only actions. Their interpretation becomes statements of principles or standards only when a means of validation exists for them.* It is the tests presented in the logical application of method which provide the substance of rationality in human conduct or in ethics.

Consider the case of the sprinter in the 100-yard dash whose coach, with the knowledge of the sprinter, has made arrangements with the official starter to permit the sprinter to leave the starting block early and not be recalled, or the athlete who has trapped the ball rather than clearly catching it and who, rather than admitting it, places the decision into the hands of the official with the attitude of "that's what the official is being paid for." In spite of pressures from external sources (the coach, the team, the fans), the element of choice of decision or action is often present with the performer. To recognize that choices can be made entails some method of validation, that is, the asking of questions as to what is right. Choosing always suggests a basis of action upon which a test of inquiry as to why this way and not another can be applied. A moral obligation entails some means of validation whereby one's actions can be appraised and evaluated. It is evident that a different response can be given and sometimes is expressed wherein the performer had no choice or choices because of acting under compulsion from external forces.

Examples may be observed in instances where the rules of the game direct behavior judgments for both the performer and the official. Regardless of how one would prefer to respond, the rules which dictate action permit little or no choice. Thus, one is not in a position to apply any means of validation and, therefore, claims a freedom from responsibility. Others than the performer who do make the decisions are the claimants to choices and, therefore, carry the moral responsibility of having their actions appraised and evaluated.

Importance of Validation

A first point of importance is that validation (the weighing of choices in ethical responsibility) lies at the heart of a method wherein appraisal and evaluation of choices may be made. It is a disturbing experience to observe, in the physical education and sport experience, those performers who prefer not to make choices or seem not to recognize the need for personal or group censure. Instead, the process of validation of decisions or actions is transferred to others, such as the teacher, coach, official, or fans (public expectations). Ethical judgments without a means of validation are generally without moral significance, and herein lies the central factor in the method proposed in this text. The blind and uncritical acceptance of a rule or mode of behavior or action taken on the basis of an absolute principle without regard for consequences is irrational and is equal to making no choice at all.

A second point of importance in a method of ethics is that a form of justification or validation of ethical decisions or judgments must involve questioning as to rightness or goodness of such decisions. Without this element in the methodology, true

Figure 4. The most symbolic of official's judgments related to unethical behavior in sports. The validation of decision involves questioning as to its rightness. (Photo courtesy of United Press International, Inc.)

validation is absent. Ross[31] states that every value judgment can, in principle, be validated, that it is always appropriate to seek such validation, and that when validation is denied, the judgment in question becomes arbitrary, capricious, and indefensible. Thus, the method of ethical judgment is like the method of science and differs only in method of validation.

HOW ACCOUNTABLE SHOULD ONE BE HELD TO METHOD?

To the extent that a person applies a method which provides alternative choices in moral responsibility and a means of validation in ethical judgment, the individual in making decisions or taking actions is less censurable. Decisions are more acceptable when carefully weighed with concern and directed toward beneficial consequences. Conversely, an action which is unquestioned and not validated is considered irresponsible and often condemned for being thoughtless. The point to be made is that if an ethical method constructed with the proper elements of choice and validation can be placed into a position to direct thinking in matters involving human conduct, the individual should be held accountable for applying its basic ingredients. To a large degree, the individual is held accountable for logical analysis and weighing of consequences when such questions are asked as, "How did she or he ever arrive at such a decision?" or "Whatever was in the mind of the person to have caused her or him to act that way?" We always seem to judge in a negative way those who do not consider alternatives or who do not even seem to recognize a need for them.

The accountability of a person to apply to the decision process a rational, methodic, and validatable procedure is no more than to prevent blind action and loss of control over what should be consciously controlled and well-directed thinking.

Flexible Versus Absolute Adherence to Method

The questions that arise, however, are these: To what degree must one adhere to a prescribed method? Might there be some flexibility in selecting alternatives based upon the circumstances in the situation? Must one be bound by the absolute rule? The answer to these questions may very well place the subject of accountability to a method in a somewhat different light.

Questions such as those presented in the preceding paragraph focus upon step seven in the prescribed method rather than upon the method as a whole. This Step indicates that selection of the alternative that proves most valid and whose consequences lead to the better or best course of action in terms of right should be made. The degree of accountability to a prescribed method is greater when the decision is to be made by a single individual, that is, when one acts alone without regard for the judgments of others. There is more flexibility when the final selection of an alternative must be made by two or more individuals or groups of individuals, each of whom may possess a somewhat different scale of values related to a specific issue.

An example of the complexity of being accountable may be cited in the instance of physical education curriculum development or revision of an existing curriculum. What should be included in the curriculum for the undergraduate major in physical education? More difficult, what should be included or excluded in a situation where there are a limited number of semester or quarter hours available within which to plan the curriculum? Should there be required courses, elective courses, or no certain specific theory courses at all? Should there be provision for election of a limited number of physical skill and methods of teaching skills courses from among a category of activities rather than an enrollment in all or most actitivies? Should all available hours be utilized for the special field, or should some provision be made for electives to be freely used as the student wishes?

These types of questions and issues reach into the basic roots of one's philosophy concerning important educational values related to the preparation of professional personnel. They can become a source of conflict whose resolve becomes a matter of alternate approaches and increased flexibility in the application of method.

There is such a variance in thought concerning *what should be* the decisions or actions of humans because of the extensive variability of human characteristics. It is extremely difficult, if not impossible, to control the interrelation of human variables. The wide variety of ethical theories which deal with human conduct and the constant change in human attitudes toward life and living attest to this fact. The selection of any alternative choice of action that proves to be most valid and whose consequences lead to the better, right, or good may need to be tempered by factors requiring a degree of flexibility rather than strict adherence to a structured method.

No formula answer can be given to questions in situations in which the situations are different. Often persons must judge the principles they live by and, too often, they do so in an absolute and therefore irrational way. There may not be one answer.

Conflicts in Seeking Unanimity in Agreement

Conflicts between moral principles and circumstances are seldom conducive toward a *perfect* resolution. However, a person may reach a valid decision in terms of his or her own personal choice after applying the elements of a validated method but may still choose wrongly in terms of someone else or in terms of a later alternative decision. One may say, "I did what I decided was proper, but if I had my chance again or had to react, I'd do it differently today under present circumstances."

There may not be unanimity in decisions regarding ethical issues. There exist differences among people concerning their feelings and thoughts related to what should have been done or what should be done. One must do the best that can be done in full moral awareness and evaluation. Complete justification of moral actions may be difficult. Conflicting alternatives may be equally justifiable, and either action may be equally valid.

Officials in sports often remove themselves from moral judgments. They enforce the rules as absolute actions without regard for intent from those who may cause violations of the rules. A football quarterback even under instructions may intentionally engage in a long count as a means of causing the opponents to move in an offside violation and thus be penalized. The officials may suspect the intent, but their task is not to perform judgments based on moral intent. Thus, they claim freedom from moral judgment. The player or coach also claims freedom from ethical responsibility because of actions that are permitted which do not violate stated rules yet do infringe upon the spirit of the rules. Such persons repudiate the fact of being moral individuals and ignore a sense of accountability. There is perhaps no more prevalent example of the shirking of ethical responsibility in physical education and sport than that found in the justification of behavior explained as "everyone else is doing it." If basketball practice, by its published rules, is to start on October 15, a variety of means are employed to start practice in September under the justification that everyone else is doing it. The list of examples of such thinking, devoid of a validated approach to proper action, is lengthy. It exists not only in the fields of physical education and athletics, but in life in general.

The point to be made is that if ethical decisions are to be made, they should be performed within the framework of a method which is interrogative and which directs judgments toward the rightness and goodness of outcomes. Fundamental to ethical judgment is interrogation and a method of appraising possible replies. It is always legitimate to ask, after a moral judgment has been made, for some form of justification or validation. Every value judgment or principle can be validated. It is appropriate to seek such validation, for without it judgments or decisions become indefensible, arbitrary, and capricious. Thus, we see that the method of moral judgment, in this respect, is like the method of science. They differ only in their means of validation.

Our concern for accountability of persons to a method must consider the existence of diversity of opinions among people. As each person is brought to the point of making a final choice among alternatives, it is possible that each person using carefully considered and rational methods of evaluation may be led to different conclusions on the same question. The weighing of choices influenced by differences in human factors, and hence opinions, does not imply that the final choice selected will be arbitrary or capricious. One may not achieve unanimity of judgment in ethical decisions as is the case in equating reason with judgment in science. Yet one must be unremitting in one's efforts to seek for validation of judgments.

The lack of unanimity or agreement in judgment in moral analysis even with principles of evaluation is recognized. There will always be some who cannot condone a seemingly completely responsible act or decision.

For example, a refusal to permit substitutions of educational offerings to students in place of others which possess entirely different objectives may be condemned out of expediency or out of differences in educational priorities. Physical education often experiences requests to excuse students from its classes in order to accommodate a program of pompon practice or for the band under the justification that the substituted activities involve physical activity and "isn't that what physical education is?" Decisions as to what is good or right for students in terms of their inclusion in the school curriculum has in recent years undergone adjustment. What was once considered extremely important and, therefore, required from a personal and humanitarian view has undergone a softening process in which individuals may now make their own decisions as to what is good or right for them in their present and future lives.

An interesting example of the application of judgment related to the prescription of activities in the college physical education program based upon what was considered good and important for students was the requirement of a beginners' swimming course for all who could not swim. A few institutions pronounced that failure to meet the beginning swimming standards would result in detention of the college degree. This practice has been influenced by change brought about by increased emphasis on the individual's rights to make decisions affecting personal welfare on the basis of one's conscious determination or free will within the context of the concept of democratic freedoms.

The Person, Not Method, Is Accountable

Hence, one of the fundamental characteristics of ethical or moral decisions is that an action or a decision which is the consequence of a rational and determinate method may not be valid by the standards of another person who judges it. It may even undergo alteration at a future date by the person who makes the present judgment. The method itself is not to be held accountable for infallible judgments. There are too many factors responsible for variability in selection of the chosen alternative. But it can be pointed out that while a person may not be considered praiseworthy or virtuous by all who view the judgment or who are affected by it, it is notable that a method of evaluation has been applied, that all possible alternatives and their consequences have been comparatively evaluated, and that the risks have been considered. The application of a method, no matter how rational or well structured, or interrogative, may not be sufficient to absolutely guarantee validity or eliminate totally the chance of mistakes.

The person who seeks direction for decision making will find a method of ethical judgment to be a desirable source for assistance. It provides the possibilities of the best choice under the circumstances and in terms of oneself. In this sense, it provides for autonomy and a reliable source for claiming responsibility. There is no need to plead ignorance of the facts or of a sense of direction, or rely upon overwhelming passion or causal inefficacy. The person will take into account knowledge of consequences of actions, a relegation of passions, present and expected feelings as a part of moral decision making, and a calculation of means and ends. The person should be aware of the consequences of responsibility in terms of the approbation of others or as a recipient of their punishments. One may fail, but the failure will be one of responsible judgment and action rather than irresponsibility, negligence, or abandonment.

The method which is suggested in this text is intended to provide the student with assurance and the validity of one's actions through a comprehensiveness in approach before the urgencies of circumstance. One does not ask to be relieved of responsibility in judging, but instead one faces it forthrightly and undivided. I must make the decision, and I do so in full consciousness of the responsibility being mine and because I know fully what I am and act as I must. To be sure, the application of a method requires practice. One doesn't resort to a notebook with the expectations of applying a methodic approach each time an ethical conflict presents itself. Individual and group practice is essential until one masters the essential steps which provide for a rational, deliberate, and unending interrogative approach, without discursive control.

DISCUSSION TOPICS AND ETHICAL INCIDENTS

1. Why are there difficulties in securing acceptance of principles which issue from philosophical concepts as contrasted with principles which derive from science? (p. 32.)

2. Apply the criteria for making a decision for rightness (right conduct) to the following incident. After having done so, ask yourself, Does the decision comply with the definition of a principle in terms of its implication for right and good from an ethical sense in promoting value for people in terms of their educational and personal welfare? (pp. 33-35.)

The swimming pool is seventy-five feet by thirty-five feet in dimension. The boys' team schedules varsity practice from 3:30 PM to 5:00 PM daily. The girls must find whatever times they can when the pool is available. A decision is made to establish another practice period from 6:30 AM to 8:00 AM daily and to rotate boys' and girls' practice schedules within the two established practice schedules every three weeks.

3. Why are decisions more apt to be right when subjected to disciplined thinking through the application of elements of a method than would decisions derived from the so-called Monday-morning-quarterback type of thinking? For example, the coach could have inserted in the latter part of the game the player who, even though possessing a head injury, would have made the best effort to secure the first down (pp. 37-38.)

4. When a sports performer contemplates on the desirability of

winning the conference championship and consequently a qualification to the national event, he or she might be tempted to resort to external sources for support (such as the use of drugs) in addition to the natural training and conditioning process. What benefits can reflective thinking in such a situation yield to the performer in clarifying the problem and in providing enlightened judgment? (pp. 41-42.)

5. Write out a description of your own for an ethical incident involving the violation of training rules by some members of a sports team to be later discovered by the coach. List as many tentative hypotheses (alternative decisions or actions) as you can that might be considered to resolve the situation based upon all the available facts.

6. If Kant's *Categorical Imperative* were to be applied to permitting fans to interrupt contests, to condoning the neglect of teaching in favor of an emphasis on coaching, or to the supporting of a boys' program of sports to the imbalancing of the girls' sports program, what could be the predicted result to physical education and sport programs universally? (p. 53.)

7. The extensive variability in human characteristics (individual differences) is evidenced in the wide variety of ethical theories and in changing attitudes toward life. For this reason flexibility rather than strict adherence in applying a method to ethical judgment and principle construction is thought best. What, then, can be expected to be a logical approach to decision making in a situation involving the *professional* versus *personal* rights of teachers and coaches? For example, how accountable should one be held to a method for arriving at a decision related to the retention of employment of a highly dedicated and effective teacher-coach who is a known homosexual? (p. 66.)

8. It may not be expected that there will be unanimity of agreement in judgment or ethical analysis even when a method of ethical judgment is applied. What, for example, would be your opinion concerning a school requirement that all students who cannot swim *must* enroll in and complete a beginning swimming class before graduation?

9. Where would you expect to find strong support in terms of

substantial data fields of knowledge (psychology, sociology, law, theology, deductive logic, science, etc.) for your decision to equally divide the practice time available in the only gymnasium in your school to both the girls' and boys' basketball teams? The boys' team has been conference champions and state finalists and has been consistently and highly supported by the local community. So, the following questions should be answered: On what grounds is my judgment correct? What evidence is there that my decision is a substantially right one? (pp. 57-58.)

10. How valid would the answer, "Because that's the way I feel, " be to the question, "Why do you neglect your teaching responsibilities in order to devote more time and energy to your coaching duties?" Or consider the answer, "It's up to the official to make the decision, not me," to the question, "Did you actually catch the ball or did you trap it?" To be valid, to what criteria must these answers be subjected? (pp. 61-64.)

11. Consider the following ethical incidents. Relative to each incident perform the following: (1) indicate alternative courses of action or decisions, (2) compare the consequences of the alternatives in terms of right, and (3) decisively select the decision or action to be taken and support your decision.

A. After studying the medical history of head injuries of an outstanding high school football player, the college team physician strongly recommends to the college head football coach not to invest the scholarship funds, time, and effort into recruiting the student-athlete. The physician also offers constructive suggestions of guidance for the student in an effort to assist the student and prevent the reoccurrence of serious injuries. In spite of the physician's advice, the football coach proceeds to recruit the student.

B. Disciplinary actions taken by physical education teachers have long been diverse and sometimes questionable in value. This particular case cites an incident wherein a senior boy student harrassed a sophomore during the physical education class in the gym while the teacher was in a nearby office. The teacher, upon returning to the gym, observed part of the incident and decided to reprimand the "bully" (as he called the senior) and teach him a lesson in proper ethical behavior. He took the senior into the small equipment room nearby, both put on boxing gloves, and they punched it out away from the view of other students. The teacher emerged from the room looking as when he entered, while the student showed signs of having taken a physical beating. The result of this disciplinary action was effective inasmuch that the senior was never again seen to harrass another student. The educational effect of such a practice on other students in physical education classes was questionable.

C. A student had failed the psychology course at the end of the fall semester. The result was an insufficient number of semester hours passed to maintain eligibility for participation on the gymnastic team during the following semester. The psychology teacher, on appeal from the student and coach, refused to change the failing grade in any way, including changing it to an incomplete. The coach consulted the athletic director. Both agreed that the student's name would be submitted as having been enrolled in the athletic director's class which was taught in the fall semester. The grade would be an *A*. The intention was that the student would attend the class taught by the athletic director in the following semester and thus complete the course at that time. The student expressed some concern, but this feeling was replaced by satisfaction and relief that eligibility for competition was achieved.

D. It was the high school pre-season try-outs in gymnastics in order to determine who would be selected as members of the varsity gym team. Cindy and Sharon were trying for the last spot on the tumbling team. Their abilities were very close and the selection outcome would be uncertain. Cindy had a bad habit of veering in a direction off the tumbling mat because of faulty hand placement in the "round-off." Cindy failed to diagnose the problem, thinking that the problem was caused by her back handspring. Sharon clearly saw and understood the cause of the problem, realizing that the fault was easily correctable. She also understood that if she volunteered to assist Cindy, it would result in an improved performance for Cindy and would be an excellent means of beating her (Sharon) out of a chance to make the varsity team.

12. The following ethical incidents in physical education and sport provide questions which are directly related to the need to interpret right from wrong. Write out your own answers to the questions after you provide reflective thought to the incidents. Then compare your answers to those of other members in the class during discussion periods established for this purpose.

A. How would you criticize the following statement? "If the practices employed by coaches and players in order to improve the chances of having winning teams are not opposed by the school administrators, public, and students, then such practices are O.K., that is, *right*." Can you distinguish between what people think is right and what is *really* right? What is the basis for making the distinction, if you feel you can do so?

B. The people of a community exert pressure on the school board to release the high school basketball coach because the coach cannot produce better than a 500 percentage average record on wins and losses. How do you judge the decisions or opinions of the community people based upon this reasoning? Provide similar illustrations of such decisions involving right or wrong based upon your own experience and observations.

C. A competitive swimmer, during the backstroke event, failed to touch the end of the pool with the hand on turning. The turn judge is only fairly certain of what occurred. The outcome of the judge's decision will decide the meet result. The judge, after the event, asks the swimmer, "Did you touch the wall with your hand on the third turn?" The swimmer, conscious of the effect of the reply, yields an answer. What would have been your answer had you been the swimmer? Why would you have answered as you did?

D. Coach Smith, shortly after committing the last available athletic scholarship (grant-in-aid) to a student, suddenly discovers the application and availability of an exceedingly superior performer. The coach attempts to figure out every possible way to regain the award so as to secure the most recent applicant. What would be your advice to the coach in this instance? On what ethical grounds do you present your advice?

E. The basketball team is nearing the opening game of the

season. The starting line-up is complete with the exception of the center spot. Two very capable players are under consideration for the position. One player, however, has considerably more playing experience, which is felt to be a decided advantage over the other. The inexperienced player approaches the coach the morning of the day of the game and issues an ultimatum. Either the player is started in the center position that night or the player definitely quits the team. As the coach reflects momentarily on this expression of intent, the thought occurs to him that both players are valuable to the team because of the obvious advantages of maintaining a good back-up center. What alternative decisions are there, and what should the coach's decision be?

F. Make a list of the ethical incidents which you have experienced or observed in physical education and sport in which the decisions or actions taken were wrong from your view. Were they wrong for the same reasons? If there might have been different reasons, indicate them. Place the incidents into categories based upon the reasons indicated. Into which category do the greatest number of incidents fall?

G. Good sportsmanship provides consideration for others (coaches, players, officials, fans) as one would wish to receive consideration and thus bring harmony into human relations. Do you agree? What is the relationship, if any, of ethics to this concept? What is the relationship of the concept of sportsmanship to situations in which persons seek advantage of their opponents in order to improve the chance of winning?

H. Roosevelt High School lost the second game of the state basketball tournament because the team's most valuable player was not permitted to play. The coach benched the player because of poor sportsmanship behavior displayed during the first tournament game: The player, on becoming emotionally upset, had sworn and made obscene gestures at the officials. There were those who condemned the disciplinary actions of the coach as being wrong. There were others who praised the coach's actions as being right. What do you mean when you indicate an action as wrong? When you indicate the action as good or right, what meaning do you intend? How would you have judged the coach's action and decision in this case?

I. The referee of a tennis match calls a decision in your favor and you know the decision is wrong. Should you protest the decision in favor of your opponent, or should you take an action which will even the score at this point? Discuss a similar situation in baseball or softball when a mistaken decision is made at a critical moment which gives you an unfair advantage over your opponent.

J. Suppose one of your close friends finds sport to be boring or declares physical education to be nonessential. What would you do and say to convince him or her that these areas of endeavor are good? How can you both, in this instance, contrast between what is good and what is not good?

Chapter 3

A SEARCH FOR PRINCIPLES FROM SELECTED ETHICAL SYSTEMS

THE fundamental ethical views that have been selected for presentation represent the writings of some of the best thinkers of humankind. The basic motivations of all persons, whatever their goals or endeavors in life, find expression in the ethical theories related to the pursuit of happiness, the devotion to duty, the struggle for power and wealth, the full development and realization of self, and authoritarianism. While these theories are constantly susceptible to modification and adjustment in accordance, with the shifting social, economic, political, and religious forces of a changing society, the basic theme of each can be applied to the times and lives of people today.

GENERAL APPLICATION OF THEORIES

Ethical theories, although often intrinsically interesting, can sometimes be irrelevant until one applies them to a practical situation or problem. They will then be found to be invaluable to assist in answering such questions as, How ought I to act? What am I to do?

There are about us all kinds of situations in which these theories are applicable. This is especially true in the physical education and athletic experience. Some examples of these situations involve power struggles among sport groups in order to secure a better measure of control, duty related to one's personal commitment to oneself and team, the use of the physical education and sport experience in the role of better finding oneself, the development of all of one's capacities for personal growth and development, and the happiness and satisfaction that comes from expending effort in achieving a goal.

Physical education and sports do not represent a superficial schematism of life. They reflect problems and issues of a type which approximates those which have to be met in the real life of all humans. If people become complacent they will not reflect on comparative values, if they do reflect with no consequent actions when actions seem needed toward achieving what is right and good, then they become decadent. Fundamental assumptions need to be challenged, and the responses to challenge need a firm base of theoretical and substantive content for support. One cannot, for example, take a stand on the role of discipline as a factor which is necessary for success in the competitive sports experience and as a necessary factor in achieving one's goals in life until the question of whether self-discipline is consistent with one's larger view of the philosophy of life and the role of oneself in it.

The problem of formulating justification for what one does in life, in making decisions or taking actions in situations which involve the welfare of oneself and of others, must ultimately be faced by each person. It is not enough to accept typical or majority points of view or to feel that, "This is the way that everyone feels or thinks," and then conform to a concensus of thought. One should be capable of developing his or her own personal philosophy about what *should be*. One should develop what are uniquely one's own basic answers to ethical problems. The opportunities to do this will be based upon a background of the best and most applicable theories and a reflection that results in a summation of one's basic attitudes, ideals, and standards.

We will later learn that one of the essential characteristics of a profession is the ability of its personnel to perform a theoretical analysis of the nature of people as well as their activities. The ability to modify conclusions derived from that analysis requires a grasp of the concepts contained within a theoretical structure of knowledge pertaining to ethics. For example, a code of ethics which supports, on the part of physical education teachers and coaches, a commitment to students not to exclude them or deny benefits to them or grant advantages to any one of them based on race, creed, color, national origin, marital status, political or religious beliefs, family, social or cultural background, or sexual orientation must find its roots in ethical theory.

Moreover, a study of ethical theories may assist one to better clarify an issue by singling out separate, different, and related but confusing questions about the issue. For example, a person who is considering whether or not to morally support highly accelerated and over-emphasized programs of intercollegiate sport may come to distinguish a number of provocative value questions.

As a potential high school coach, what part would you play in helping a highly talented athlete (boy or girl) cope with the high-power recruiting techniques employed by some college coaches? As a college coach, what would be your price for winning? How does the pressure used by college recruiters on blue chip high school athletes affect your attitude toward college sports?

One may be confronted with determining the extent to which he or she must compromise moral concepts and ideals related to what is thought to be right in terms of educational values and practices with those values and practices which are sometimes observed in such accelerated programs. For example, these questions may center upon (1) whether winning should be considered as the *only* means of judging success; (2) whether participation in sports serves as an adjunct vehicle which supplements, supports, and contributes to the values which educational programs are intended to impart; (3) whether the financial supporting structure for sports programs is commensurate with and proportionate to other educational programs within the institution; (4) whether the practices of student-athletes' recruitment and subsidization are in accord with established rules of educationally based or recognized and approved institutional organizations; (5) whether academic admission and retention standards and curricula adjustments should be conditioned so as to favor privileged groups of students; (6) whether coaches should be evaluated in terms of educational goals rather than commercial objectives as wins and losses, money taken at the gate, or publicity accorded to teams, individuals, or the institution on the field of play; (7) whether sports departments should operate as separate units apart from the operational structure of other departments; and (8) whether coaches should be employed primarily on the basis of their ability to produce winning teams rather than as bona fide members of the faculty with educational responsibility who are provided faculty benefits.

SPECIFIC APPLICATION OF THEORIES

The more specific purposes which the selected ethical theories may serve in assisting to answer questions of how one ought to decide or act may be

1. To provide for independence in thinking and encourage a flexible and adaptable attitude toward change rather than an intellectual conformity.
2. To assist in the construction of new ideas and the ability to defend these ideas.
3. To provide a base for clarifying and criticizing basic assumptions.
4. To provide a base for a reflective study of questions related to the standards of conduct which a person develops and adopts for oneself and which may then be used in making decisions and arriving at one's own statements of principles.
5. To assist in the development of some positive and explicit scheme of values that helps to give life direction and provide guidance in the solution of ethical problems.

In summary, it may be acknowledged that much of ethical theory is controversial. Normative ethics, concerned with what should be, cannot be expected to provide a complete listing of ethical principles, nor may the principles that are provided be expected to be acceptable to all persons. One must develop his or her own principles that serve one's own purposes and which are consonant with one's own established views of life. A person can only arrive at his or her own acceptable list of criteria on which to formulate judgments and, after having critically evaluated these, develop principles which are based upon a tenable system of ethical beliefs.

CLASSIFICATION OF ETHICAL THEORIES

Prior to a presentation of selected ethical systems, it is well to secure a perspective of ethical theories in general. The amount of literature which deals with this subject is very large. Although there are wide divergencies in views expressed in the theories, there are also some common elements.

Abelson and Friquegnon[1] indicate that the history of ethical philosophy is a continuous dialogue between progressively more refined forms of ethical absolutism and ethical relativism. The students of the ethical study experience may find themselves forming decisions as to the right rules of conduct somewhere along the continuum.

The absolutist will take the side of right or wrong, independent of any conditions; the relativist will allow judgments to be influenced by social and individual needs, customs, and other factors. Abelson and Friquegnon therefore, cite four major classifications of ethical theories: (1) religious absolutism (right is obedience to divine commands); (2) conventionalism (right is dependent on laws, customs, and agreements of the social group); (3) rational absolutism (right is deducted from the concept of reason and the principles are applied universally and unconditionally to all persons and in all situations without regard for cultural backgrounds or personal needs); and (4) utilitarian relativism (right is judged in accordance to the degree to which an action produces pleasure or alleviated pain for most people rather than for one or a small group of individuals).

Abelson and Friquegnon state that, while the issue between ethical absolutism and ethical relativism has not been finally resolved, the theory of utilitarian relativism conforms more closely than any other ethical theory to the common sense ways in which people arrive at their ethical decisions.

Patterson[28] also recognizes commonness and diversity among all ethical theories. Upon this recognition, he indicates that the fundamental principle of what is right or wrong issues from two divisional classes of ethical theories: (1) the *source* or way in which knowledge of the theory is obtained and (2) the *motive* or *goal* which prompts an action.

We shall draw upon both types in our search for principles related to ethical conduct in physical education and sport. The first type, related to the source or way in which we obtain knowledge of what is right or good, finds four main divisions, namely, *authoritarian, intuitional, empirical,* and *rational.*

Authoritarian ethics is based upon rules that issue from an individual or group whose authority is not questioned enough to upset the source. We title this source as *authoritarianism.*

Intuitional theories indicate that a person *knows* directly what is right or wrong in any situation. This intuitive element is an awareness, probably identified as a voice of conscience, that tells one what ought to be done.

Empirical theories are based upon rules that have been found to be good in the past and which issue from human experience. The only way the empiricist will accept the principles of truth is based on observation, experimentation, and the formulation and testing of hypotheses that *can* be verified through deductions and further observations.

Rational theories consider a doctrine of truth as reasonable when it is free from any self-contradiction and is in harmony with all known relevant facts. From this view, the theories apply as their criterion, the authority of reason. The rationalists will test any proposed theory on this basis.

The second classification of ethical theories related to the motive or goal which prompts an action consists of two groups, the *formalistic* or deontological and the *teleological.*

Formalistic theories are best demonstrated through the writings of Immanuel Kant, whose work we shall draw on to better understand the base for motives which stem from a sense of duty. Formalism, in determining the goodness of an act based on the motive which produced it, is also expressed in ethics concerned with obedience to laws of nature and obedience to commands of the deity. They attempt to answer the question, How *ought* we to act?

Teleological theories, upon which we largely depend in selecting the theories presented for our consideration, accept as the standard of right and good some particular end or goal toward which actions are directed. They attempt to answer the question, What *is* the good? The teleologist feels that the consequences as well as the motives in performing an act must be considered.

While there will always be some overlapping in the classes of theories, the ones presented here will include such titles as happiness and pleasure, the struggle for power, individual development and self-realization, the devotion to duty, and authoritarianism.

THE RELATIVITY OF ETHICS

There has been, of recent years, an increased amount of reference to the theory of ethical relativity in justifying decisions related to right conduct. There has been a veering from obedience as a norm, be it custom, law, or external authority, and a movement toward reflective criticism. Rapid and extensive technological and social change has broadened viewpoints toward life and interpersonal relations. While there have been noticeable shifts in moral standards, personal and social life has more persistently revolved about morals as they relate to human feelings, intelligence, and life experiences. As a consequence, there has been a decided move away from rigidity, fixed customs, and group morality toward a strongly taken position on human rights and human values, and an assertion of the role of the individual consistent with the principles inherent in a democratic society.

The conduct of participants in physical education and sport in recent years has been somewhat consistent with the movement toward increased freedom of expression. In its earlier stage of development, the movement constituted a source of conflict between the personal freedoms demanded by the participants and the disciplinary rules of coaches and teachers.

Grouping of Moral Standards

Titus and Keeton[39] indicate that moral standards today can be classified into three groups in accordance with those who adopt them. First, there are those who live under *codes* where an external authority such as custom, law, institution, scripture, etc., is accepted as final. These types of standards work well for a simple and fairly static society, although it is to be admitted that many thoughtful persons are successfully guided to a large extend by codes of conduct which issue from external sources.

Second, there are those who rebel against the earlier established codes because of the changing social context in which modern life has evolved. Their move has been in the direction of a rather extreme position in which acknowledgment states there is no right or wrong except as thinking, emotion, desire, or attitude determine it. This position is one which we will examine and shall indicate it as *ethical relativism.*

Third,[39] a position of *normative and reflective morality* is one claimed by those who "formulate moral judgments and control their conduct on the basis of a reflective evaluation of principles and a careful examination of facts in their relation to human life" (pp. 59-60). This approach takes into account exceptional circumstances, stresses, and new problems of today's environment. It calls for reflection upon the older ways of guidance, such as custom, law, and conscience, and asks not merely what was done in the past but what the future demands. Those who apply this method of arriving at ethical judgments would seem to be moral in a higher sense than simply following custom, law, or external authorities.

Whatever reference is made to formulate standards of ethical conduct, there is agreement that humankind can do best by bringing to bear upon thinking and reason all possible resources available in order to produce a kind of life which yields maximum benefits to all.

The Relativistic Theory

One can better understand the meaning of *ethical relativism* by placing it in contrast to the opposite kind of extreme posi-

Figure 5. A prayer for an injured opponent. A demonstration of reflective morality and the true spirit of sportsmanship based on compassion and a sensitivity for humanity — ingredients which must enoble all human endeavors. Courtesy, Illinois High School Asso.

tion called *ethical absolutism.* The absolutists claim that there is but one eternally true and valid moral code. The code applies with rigid impartiality to all. What is an obligation for one is an obligation for everyone irrespective of geographical location, time, or period. There is not one law or moral standard for one group of people and then another standard for another group. There is but one law, one standard, one morality for all people, and this standard or law is absolute and unvarying. The ethical absolutist does not object to the questioning of the validity of the moral standard. The absolutist simply declares that whatever is morally right or wrong — be it abortion, sexual promiscuity, suicide, capital punishment, war and terrorism, or euthanasia — is morally right or wrong for all people at all times. In this sense there is a single moral standard for all human beings. We shall view this in more detail when we present the theory of Kant and devotion to duty.

The ethical relativist has taken a position which represents, somewhat, a revolutionary tendency of the time in which we have been living. The chief role of the relativist has been that of a revolt against absolutism and against the rigid dogmas of conventionalism in an age of increased freedom of thought and action of the individual. Knowing that relativism is the opposite extreme from absolutism we can more easily understand the essence of the tenets of the relativist. The relativist asserts that there is not merely one moral law, one code, one standard. There are many moral laws, codes, standards. What morality expects in one place or time may be quite different from what morality expects in another place or time. Any morality is relative to the time, the place, and the circumstances in which it is found. It is in no sense absolute.

Stace,[36] who presents a comprehensive treatment of the subject of ethical relativity, including arguments in support of and against the theory, states as follows:

> The ethical relativist consistently denies, it would seem whatever the ethical absolutist asserts. For the absolutist there is a single universal moral standard. For the relativist there is no such standard. There are only local, ephemeral, and vari-

able standards. For the absolutist there are two senses of the word "standard." Standards in the sense of sets of current moral ideas are relative and changeable. But the standard in the sense of what is actually morally right is absolute and unchanging. For the relativist no such distinction can be made. There is only one meaning of the word standard, namely, that which refers to the local and variable sets of moral ideas. . . . Finally, the absolutist makes a distinction between what actually is right and what is thought right. The relativist rejects this distinction and identifies what is moral with what is thought moral by certain human beings or groups of human beings. (p. 11)

Levels of Ethical Relativism

There are various levels upon which the relativity of ethics or morals exist. For example, one may form a judgment of right action upon feelings of approval or disapproval. The judgment is simply based on how one feels or, in a sense, upon a psychological state. "This is how I feel about it, and that is sufficient for me." Accordingly, the basis of this decision is not a genuine or valid one, and it becomes impossible to decide who is right or wrong in ethical differences. This level of expression is the *emotive* level. The emotive theory provides the expression of feeling as the base in making moral judgments. Emotivism states that the purpose of moral judgment is to express emotion.

The fields of physical education and sport offer many examples of the expression of judgments of what is right or wrong based upon emotional feelings. A survey of ethical incidents in sport made in an attempt to develop a typology of ethical behavior revealed the prevalence of a high degree of emotivism in three types of situations. They were (1) where there is a mixture of an exceedingly high degree of loyalty of fans toward their own team, the contest is close, and winning is a critical factor in championship competition; (2) in traditional contests between teams who have developed intense competition and rivalry over a long period of years; and (3) in the expressions of individual athletes concerning the judgments of coaches which have directly affected the athlete, a judgment indicated as discriminatory.

The emotive level of expression which represents a type of ethical relativism is evidenced in other ways. For example, when the people of a community, including school officials, take the case of a lost game based on an official's error over the heads of the state high school association into the district court for a decision, the resultant feelings are expressed at the emotive level. When the local teacher-coach is discovered to be a homosexual, judgments are immediately based on emotional feelings. When the parents of little league baseball or pee-wee basketball harass officials and coaches, educational standards and objectivity are abandoned. When the fans get into violent contact with other fans, players, and officials, moral perspectives are lost.

There is a second kind of relativistic base called the *egoistic* level. Whatever is morally good is relative to whatever is considered in one's best interest. This type of expression is quite prevalent today, although philosophers do not make a great effort to substantiate it. The educational approach to curriculum design by including in the educational program those elements considered good for students has often been challenged by the individual who rebels against requirements related to subject experience and states, "I'll decide what is good for me in light of my own planned future and what I feel in life is important to me." This reaction is sometimes evident in relation to the previously cited requirement related to beginning swimming classes in physical education. The decision as to what is right and good for the individual will be decided by each person, regardless of whatever humanitarian values are involved for both the individual and the society.

A third type of ethical relativism called *cultural* relativism operates on a social base. The standards which exist are those which are derived from the values of a particular group within a particular culture. What is morally right in one culture may be morally wrong in another. Unlike the emotive or egoistic levels of operation, cultural relativism offers a more objective base in the form of group or social agreement, be it custom or convention. Ethically approved standards are aligned with what is in accord with customs, mores, or socially approved ways of acting in the particular cultural group. Here there is no absolute or universal or transcendent ethical standard. This type of expression is often found in the expectation of behavior of persons in professional groups and is found in their professional codes of conduct. Teachers, laywers, doctors, government officials, scientists, etc., often define their expected actions in a moralistic sense. These are expressions of ethical judgments, that is, judgments which differ from other groups.

Codes of conduct are constantly evaluated so as to change with the changing times. This fact does not mean to imply that there is a universality of content in the codes of professional groups. Although there is a great deal of similarity rather than diversity in the general approach to responsibilities and obligations to both the group and to the society which are served by the group, there are a sufficient amount of differences which reflect a relativity in value judgments.

In summary, the theory of relativism holds that there is no absolute morality, that persons differ in what they think is right, that circumstances affect what is right, and that standards of judgment are related to human feeling and thinking and reside in the context of the time, place, and conditions affecting the ethical judgment to be made. As the conditions of life change, as society and its people make progress in knowledges, in human insights concerning the welfare of people, in social relationships and human understanding, and in increased standards of living, changes will also occur in moral and ethical codes.

I. AUTHORITARIANISM

An authoritarian type of social structure is one in which strict rules of conduct are decreed and enforced by those in power. Having previously made a comparison between absolutism and relativism so as to clarify the meaning of concepts, we might in this instance take a comparative view of authoritarianism and its counterpart, democracy.

A democratic society provides opportunities for individuals to compete on equal terms, thus constituting a different view of morality, a view in which the rules of conduct represent a concensus among equals and are not promulgated by a superior authority. The essential element in democratic procedure is that of equality in opportunities for deliberation with the resulting action or decision based on the majority vote or, in specific instances, added protection for the minority by the two-thirds rule. The central core of the democratic concept is recognition and support for the individual person whose dignity and rights as a human being are upheld through democratic processes. Individuals participate in the formulation of rules, policies, or principles which affect their lives and their living.

Authoritarianism Versus Individual Democracy

Pepper[29] demonstrates two opposite directions in which lines of moral legislation may proceed. One is based on the dynamics of survival and is found in authoritarianism or political socialism. The other, based on purposive drives, is found in an individualistic democracy. In both of these ethical systems, the need for the individual to seek personal satisfactions, desires, and freedoms and the need of the individual to exist as a member of a social species intent on survival, propagation, and maximum security are empirically well authenticated. Contrasting elements within the systems are presented by Pepper as the following:

Functional Authoritarian Society

1. Survival as dominant motive.
2. Basic right of society over individuals
3. Centralization in government.
4. Efficiency as chief aim of social organization.

5. Discipline or team play as social attitudes sought.
6. Duty or loyalty as personal attitudes sought.

Individualistic Democratic Society

1. Happiness as dominant motive.
2. Basic right of individuals as instrumental view of society.
3. Decentralization in government.
4. Opportunity for individual enterprise and satisfaction as aim of social organization.
5. Initiative or tolerance as social attitudes sought.
6. Satisfaction or compromise as personal attitudes sought.

Religious Authoritarianism

Strict authoritarianism, requiring uncritical conformity, provides no democratic process in arriving at decisions for what is right for self or others. Authoritarianism might be better seen in terms of what is probably its oldest concept, that is, the religious view that the meaning of right is obedience to divine commands.

The religious conception of right as obedience to the commands of a superior being is based upon the belief that all processes of life reflect the will of their Creator and that conscience is the voice of God in the human soul. Robert C. Mortimer,[23] in defending this view, maintains that natural law, personal conscience, and church pronouncements are the agencies for interpreting revelations and discovering what God commands us to do. An act is right, he maintains, "because God commands it." Parental authority, which is the original standard of ethical judgment for the child (until the child later performs his or her own evaluation of conduct, including that of parents), is somewhat an extension of the religious concept of divine authority. The question of whether the rightness of divine commandments can be determined by fundamental ethical standards lies at the center of the controversy between religious and secular ethics.

Conventional Authoritarianism

A less severe form of authoritarianism is that which regards the validity of rules of conduct as dependent upon statutory laws, customs, or formalistic and strictly structured agreements. We may term these processes as those within the concept of conventional authoritarianism.

Although these processes permit some degree of participatory action by those whose lives are directed by them, they are, nevertheless, issued by authority and provide for sanctions in the event of noncompliance to the commands. Neither religious nor so-called conventional authoritarianism permits rational criticism of the prevailing rules of conduct. Abelson and Friquegnon[1] point out that "ethical judgment in both types of views arrives at a point beyond which one can no longer reason about what is right or wrong, but can only insist: that is the law or custom of our society, or that is what God has commanded, and, therefore, right by definition" (p. 17). Both require an uncritical conformity to social authority and custom. Both imply that ethical reasoning must terminate with an appeal to an authority whose might makes his or her decisions right.

The processes of conventional authoritarianism may be witnessed in the application of the rules and policies employed by sport groups whether they function in an institutional setting, in a conference, or under a national organization. The rules for the sport group may be formulated within the institution by the athletic committee and approved by the Board of Trustees. They may be established by members of the conference, or they may be developed by an executive committee on a national association for approval of the membership. Instances of such national organizations in athletics would be the National Collegiate Athletic Association, the Association for Intercollegiate Athletics for Women, the National Association for Intercollegiate Athletics, and the National Federation of High School Athletic Associations.

The Essential Element for Effective Authority

The tenets of authoritarianism are apt to be found in situations where there is a unanimous acceptance by the group of an objective or objectives held to be of paramount importance above all others. An extreme manifestation of such an objective would be that of survival of the individual or group. A typical example which comes to mind is that of the lifeboat filled with men, women, and children adrift on the open sea following a shipwreck in which all were willing to accept the authority of the ship's officer in establishing a survival pattern of behavior. This pattern of behavior is often referred to as *lifeboat ethics*. A lesser extreme would be the sports team whose members fully accede to the coach's authority as the most knowledgeable and experienced person who can successfully guide the team through to the championship of the conference or the national title.

When the survival forces are dominant, there is a need for social solidarity. There follows a highly integrated social organization toward a centralized form of political structure and a rigid pattern of binding rules of conduct. The ethical and moral rules are then fixed by the rigid rules of the authoritarian source. Discipline and loyalty to the cause are indoctrinated, and the achievement of each individual in contributing to the central goal is dominant over any personal satisfactions. Any effort by the individual toward personal gratification for its own sake may be morally condemned as wrong since it distracts the individual from duties in the fullest achievement of an assigned role in serving the welfare of the group.

In a more popular sense the application of authority toward the individual may be observed in the "shape up or ship out" concept. It may also be observed when directed toward a subsidiary group who fails to enforce its authority, causing its members to comply to recognizable *right* conduct as that conduct is interpreted by a superior group. This latter process may be observed when a national or regional educational organization (such as the American Council on Education or a regional accrediting association), dissatisfied with the educational policies and practices of its member institutions, may invoke their authority for educational change. It is also observed when state high school athletic associations take action against member schools for infractions of the rules which are designed for the educational conduct of sport programs.

Whether manifested by the teacher to the student, the coach to the athlete, or the national professional organization to its institutional members, authoritarianism as a type of structure in which the rules of conduct are enforced by those in power exists to varying degrees in many types of human relationships.

The Theory of Thomas Hobbes

One may observe reference to the tenets of authoritarianism

in the theories of some of the foremost thinkers of former periods of historical, political, and social movements. Some of these theories, and particularly that of Thomas Hobbs, turned to questions of human nature and the operational bases of human society in an effort to discover an equitable foundation upon which all people could live in harmony.

Thomas Hobbes (1588-1679) saw the need of the individual to desire the preservation of his own life, the satisfaction of his own wants, and the increase of his own power and security. Because everyone was equal and desired the same things from life, all were in a natural state of competition (a state of nature), a situation that Hobbes predicted would lead to chaos and anarchy. To escape from the state of nature, all would give up their rights except the right to life and physical liberty. The people would agree to yield all their rights to some person who would become their king or chief, dictator, or political sovereign. The simplest form of government was an absolute monarchy which would guarantee peace. Once the rights had been surrendered, there was no way to regain them except through civil war and a return to the state of nature — which was recognized as the worst of all states in life. Thus, the reign of law provided security and possibilities for greater enjoyment of life rather than killing each other in competition for them.

Under Hobbes's theory, the law as laid down by the authority of the state determined what was morally right or wrong, just and unjust. It became the business of the ruler to decide what was the common good which all citizens should promote. It was the function of the ruler to lay down the laws or norms under which all citizens pursued their ends. The common good was the good of every person, and the laws of the state were the moral laws. Authority in matters of right and wrong were not left to the interpretation provided by God's laws or individual conscience. The official interpretation would be that of the king or political sovereign. In a political society, the decrees of the sovereign defined the conditions of right action. Justice was obedience to the sovereign, and, consequently, the king could do no wrong. The sovereign thus ruled with absolute power. A person had only two recourses open: to conform outwardly to the state and keep one's scruples to oneself, or, if outward conformity would endanger immortal soul, martyrdom was available.

Hobbes recognized that law and order were the prerequisites to all culture and the higher things of life. He, therefore, contrasted man *in a state of nature* to man under *the social contract*. The critical and supreme question to be answered was, What is the best status for people as they seek the goodness of life? Hobbes founded what he thought to be the best answer based on the human's strongest passions, fear and self-preservation. Again we observe the willingness of persons to form agreements with others to follow certain rules of conduct, thus purchasing security at the price of restraints on personal freedoms.

There has been in recent years an expression of fear of an extreme movement by governments toward the philosophy expressed by Hobbes. The establishment of measures for collective goals for the social order to the neglect of those which preserve and promote individual rights has been a matter of concern. In societies which have long emphasized the concept of equal justice under the law, the concern has been that the original doctrine is being extended beyond the concept of equality of rights toward one of equality of conditions.

The guarantee of the Fourteenth Amendment that no state shall deprive any citizen of "equal protection of the laws" is a way of expressing what has been viewed as each person's inherent right of equality in freedom under the law. The American tradition has always insisted upon an equality measured in freedom, independence, and opportunity. The recognition of inequality of individual talents, with full support of the legal guarantee of equal opportunity, has led to progress in religion, intellectual affairs, the production of material wealth, and the pursuit of individual meaning in life. Many social advances have their origins in providing individuals the opportunity to give full expression to creative resources.

The establishment of an extensive system of bureaucracies, of suppression of individual and institutional creativity, and of government interference with the process of life guaranteed under a democratic existence, often under the threat of sanctions, has constituted one of the primary causes of national and international concern. The self-same practices, expressed in the concept of authoritarianism, may extend beyond the boundaries of a national government. They may permeate through the entire matrix of all human relationships, including education and the entire spectrum of sports administration.

II. THE DEVOTION TO DUTY

The important fact about ethical theories which deal with formalistic ethics is obedience to rules rather than satisfaction of desires, duty and conformity to moral laws, fulfilling the demands and obligations to which one is subjected, and doing what is *right*. The rules in terms of *shall* and *shall not* set the limits within which conduct takes place. Breaking the rules means acting disobediently, being illicit, committing a sin, or doing what is *wrong*.

For example, students of physical education classes or as members of athletic teams are expected to control their impulses, in obedience to the teaching of teachers or rules of coaches, if these impulses run counter to a type of behavior which demands discipline and, supposedly, develops good character. Athletes, realizing obligations to the team, surrender the satisfaction of personal desires.

The Kantian System

The Kantian system of ethical theory[15] has been selected to represent the central core of the presentation of devotion to duty.*

Immanuel Kant (1724-1804), the greatest philosopher of his age, was born in Konigsberg, East Prussia, a seaport on the Baltic Sea. He had a strong religious background in a faith grounded in experience of inner fervor and piety and influ-

---

*One should read the variant views of Josiah Royce on *The Religion of Loyalty,* Gilbert Murray on *The Stoic Philosophy,* and W. David Ross on *What Makes Right Actions Right* so as to gain a conception of alternatives to Kant's theory.

enced by the ethics of the Sermon on the Mount. He chose theology as his field of study in the university. In spite of his theological background, he came to ethics and philosophy by way of the sciences because of a keen interest in physics, mathematics, and metaphysics. Kant took on the task of expressing the growing ascendancy of science in the modern world and sought to achieve for ethics something of the same universality and rigor of reason which supposedly was already demonstrated in the physical sciences.

Kant recognized the capacity of man's free will to respond to the notion of moral duty, choosing to do the right rather than pursuing a different path to personal happiness. He attributed to reason the capacity not only to see the moral law but to induce the will by free choice to abide by it. For Kant, the rational will is essentially a moral will, a will to do one's duty, and it is only in this exercise of the moral will that a person is truly free. Otherwise, he or she is a slave to impulse and desire.

The Doctrine of Good

A better understanding of Kant's concept of duty requires a review of his doctrine of *good*. The most concise and effective expression of Kant's theory of the *good* is found in the opening paragraph of the *Foundations of the Metaphysics of Morals*[15], his most important work in ethics.

> Nothing can possibly be concerned in the world, or even out of it, which can be called good without qualification, except a Good Will. Intelligence, wit, judgment, and the other talents of the mind, however they may be named, or courage, resolution, perseverance, as qualities of temperament, are undoubtedly good and desirous in many respects; but these gifts of nature may also become extremely bad and mischievous of the will which is to make use of them, and which, therefore, constitutes what is called character, is not good. It is the same with the gifts of fortune. Power, riches, honour, even health, and the general well-being and contentment with one's condition which is called happiness, inspired pride, and often presumption, if there is not a good will to correct the influence of those on the mind, and with this also

to rectify the whole principle of acting, and adapt it to its end. The sight of a being who is not adorned with a single feature of a pure and good will, enjoying unbroken prosperity, can never give pleasure to an impartial rational spectator. Thus a good will appears to constitute the indispensable condition even of being worthy of happiness. (p. 9).

Thus, we can discern that a good will is good without any qualifying clauses beginning with *if* or *unless*. A rational or principled will is good simply and under all circumstances. This is not the case with other goods, such as knowledge, property, and wealth, which may be evil unless managed by a rational will. The value of one act, says Kant, lies not in the motive, intention, or good wishes; it lies in the will. These matters (motive, intention, good wishes) imply aiming at good consequences, and neither the actual nor the intended or the wished-for consequences have any direct connection with the *good will*.

Kant's Moral Law or Categorical Imperative

In order to grasp the essential meaning of Kant's unconditional Moral Law or Categorical Imperative, several modified cases involving a rule or law might be presented.

Case 1. A student upon graduation from college enters into a contract to teach and coach in a specific high school. Shortly after, the student experiences a reluctance to fulfill the contract because of being offered a higher salaried position in another school. Is it right for the student to break the contract? If the contract is broken, the student's maxim (rule) becomes, "If it is inconvenient to fulfill a contract, it is best to break it." If this maxim is applied universally, it becomes, "All contracts shall be broken, at the convenience of either party." But such a law when applied universally would be inconsistent with the whole concept of contract. There would be no point in formulating contracts because they would have no practical or legal meaning and no force.

Case 2. A sports performer and coach find it prudent to lie in order to gain a personal advantage or a possible benefit for the team. The performer must run the 200 meters in a specific established cut-off time or better in order to qualify for the national championships. The time has been achieved in practice on several occasions but not officially. The qualifying time submitted was not, therefore, official. The liar's maxim would be, "It is better to lie than to hurt the team by possibly depriving them of a chance to score points in the meet." If this lie were to be universalized, we would have a practice established which would be characterized by, "One should tell the truth with discretion, and a lie when the truth is indiscreet or when it could be harmful to others." If this practice of lying in such cases was encouraged, there would be many liars, and no person's word would be trustworthy. The result would be to undermine peoples' relations with each other and to society. Kant states that if a person must speak, the moral obligation is to tell the truth.

Case 3. A sports department of a college obligates itself to an athlete to provide a grant-in-aid in support of outstanding performances in athletics. When the performer does not meet the expectations of the department after the season of competition, the grant is withdrawn. There was no written contract for the agreement of support nor detailed conditions under which the grant could be maintained. The trust is, therefore, dissolved by the officials of the sports department. The maxim employed by the department which abused the trust would be, "An unenforceable trust is not binding." If this practice was universalized or constricted into a principle to be applied in all future cases, it would destroy the meaning of trust. The reputation of such a department would be seriously affected, and student-athletes would avoid association with it.

It may be seen that the method of testing a maxim (rule) by universalizing it provides the clue to the discovery of the *Moral Law*. It can be stated as follows: *Act on the maxim, and that maxim only, which you could will to become by your act a universal law of nature.* Kant called this law *The Moral Law* or *The Categorical Imperative.* Another manner of expressing the imperative is, "I ought never to act except in such a way that I can also will that my maxim should become a universal law."

The basic idea of duty, then, is simply that of acting in accord with general principles which one can recognize as valid for anyone and claiming no right that one does not admit as right for others also.

Conformity to universally valid principles is the end of purpose of the moral law; its sole criterion of the rightness of an action is whether it is applicable to all rational beings, and the criterion of its applicability is whether one can live in accord with the rule without contradicting oneself by adopting one rule at one time and another rule at another time.

To better understand the concept of duty implied in *The Categorical Imperative*, we might contrast a law of nature with a moral law. A law of nature was demonstrated in Chapter 2 dealing with the definition of a principle. The Newtonian Laws so often applied in the field of kinesiology to better explain the phenomena of physical movement and its relationships to total performance explain how objects or material matter behave. A moral law is not a statement of how persons *do* behave, but how they *ought* to behave. *Ought* implies duty, and if persons were not conscious of duty, there would be no *ought*. Without the moral *ought* there is no morality. A moral law, therefore, is always an imperative.

Maxim Versus Imperative

Maxim is a rule or principle that one formulates for oneself which provides guidance for conduct relative to one's goals, desires, or thoughts. It serves as a counsel of prudence for the person who formulates it and is not necessarily binding on others. The athlete may, in the drive for excellence in performance, be reminded of a maxim, "You get out of your performance exactly what you put into it." This type of maxim is a generalization of experience.

Imperatives, on the other hand, when stated unconditionally, are intended universally, are the products of reason, and, if strictly universal, are rational and objective. For example, "Thou shalt not steal" can be applied by all persons and on all occasions and is a rational law.

While a maxim is a personal rule of conduct, it can be placed into an imperative form (use of the shall or shall not), and its validity can be tested by applying it universally. If it can be applied to all rational beings under all circumstances, it may serve as a moral law.

Types of Imperatives

Another point to be noted in reference to the concept of duty implied in Kant's *Categorical Imperative* is that imperatives may be either categorical, hypothetical, or disjunctive. A categorical imperative is stated unconditionally such as is found in the statements of the Ten Commandments. A hypothetical imperative is stated with a condition usually begun by an *if* clause, such as "If you want to be a successful athlete, you must obey the laws of training," or "If you wish to receive an *A* grade in the beginning swimming course, you must swim one hundred yards," or "Wear protective pads if you do not wish to be injured in contact sports." A disjunctive imperative provides alternates indicated by *or*. For example, "Either report regularly for class instruction or drop the course," or "Either obey the rules established by the coach or you will be removed from the sport."

Categorical imperatives are binding; they have no *ifs* or *ors*. We say, therefore, that moral laws are duty binding and are not counsels of prudence as are subjective maxims.

Interpretation of the Categorical Imperative

One can interpret Kant's Categorical Imperative in two ways. First, the act of universalizing one's maxim would magnify the consequences so that one could easily see its tendency to do harm or good. For example, what may appear to be a very small wrong if only one person acted on a rule may appear as a very great wrong if everyone adopted the rule, and what seems right under exceptional circumstances may reveal its inherent wrongness if the rule is applied steadfastly in all circumstances.

Second, Kant supported the concept of rationality and consistency. If a rule, when universalized, had internal inconsistencies, it was irrational. Internal consistency rather than consequences of the rule was the best test of its worth. For example, consider the maxim that a person may tell a lie if it is felt that the truth would be harmful or indiscreet. One could never be certain that the truth was ever being told under such a maxim. No person's word would be trustworthy. The result would be an inconsistent behavior of persons in relationships with each other and would lead to an undermining of an important element in the progress of society and civilization.

Kant emphasized that actions have moral worth only if they are the product of a rational will. The fact that a person performs outwardly in conformity with the moral law is not enough; action must be directed by the moral law. One may act in a kindly and generous way and in the same outward way as indicated by the moral law, but it is of no moral worth unless the impulse is guided and supported by a rational will. In general it is not enough for a person to do the right act; one must do it for the right reason and with the right will.

This proposition, when applied to physical education and sport, raises interesting questions. Do the performers respond in the sense of doing what is considered morally right and in conformance with recognized moral law out of a sense of the need to adhere to the rules of the sport and games or from an inner sense of conforming to a rational and good will? Is it the influence of the rules and the enforcement of the rules with resultant penalties or sanctions in the event of rule infractions that produces overt behavior, or does the behavior of performers follow out of adherence to a moral recognition of the concept of sportsmanship and fair play based on moral grounds?

Desires, goals, and wants may not be grounded in rational will but are subjective. All such things as wealth, pleasure, power, and honor are private wishes. All must be brought under the will and subjected to reason. They must be regulated by principles and ultimately by the Moral Law. Right and desire may coincide, but it can never be right to do what one desires because one desires it. Duty is the one which is right whenever right and desire are in conflict.

III. PLEASURE AND HAPPINESS AS THE BASE

The ethical theory based upon the pursuit of happiness is said to conform most closely with common sense ways in which people arrive at their ethical decisions. The concept when viewed as a basic human right and as the ultimate answer to questions of ethics has been shown to be one of the greatest liberalizing forces in ethical and political movements. It finds an expression in the governing documents of free societies, particularly in those of a democratic nation. It formed the foundation of thought and ideas in the famous defenses of liberty written by John Locke, Thomas Jefferson, and John Stuart Mill. The primary concept supported by these thinkers was that the common happiness of all people is the proper guiding principle of government, and they proclaimed the right of the individual to be free and pursue his or her own happiness in one's own way.

There is a variety of literature which deals with happiness and pleasure as the primary end or goal in life. We shall approach the various ethical theories which treat this subject by first looking at the doctrines of *hedonism*. We will then concentrate our attention on the ethical theory of *utilitarianism* and attempt to place it into a position so as to bear upon the processes of ethical decisions in physical education and sport.

Happiness or pleasure (these terms are used interchangeably in this presentation) as the end or goal of action in seeking a standard for what is good contrasts rather sharply with the formalistic theory of Kant, which finds meaning for good in duty and obedience to rules prescribed for humans to follow. Here one looks to the end or goal (the teleological view which looks to the end or consequences of an action to determine its rightness or wrongness, its goodness or badness) and asks, Is the goal found in the personal consciousness of the doer, or does it lie outside the person and is good regardless of any pleasure derived from it?

The Hedonist Doctrines

This question is answered by the hedonist (one holding to the doctrine that pleasure is the only good and pain is the only evil) who asserts that the goodness of an act is always determined by the amount of pleasure or happiness derived from it. One may have in mind the immediate pleasure for the individual, the greatest amount of pleasure in one's life as a whole, or the greatest amount of pleasure for the greatest number of persons.

There seems to be much support for this view inasmuch that the element common to all actions recognized as being good is pleasure or happiness. Happiness can justifiably be an end in itself. One may pursue money, reputation, or power in order to secure pleasure or happiness, but one does not pursue these ends in order to obtain some other end. These facts seem to indicate that happiness is the essential element in goodness and points up the principle that an act is only good when it contributes toward happiness.

The hedonist doctrine has usually been associated with some form of empirical tradition in philosophy. Empiricists believe that all knowledge is derived from experience, and therefore moral ideals cannot be based on the authority of any person, not even of a supernatural being. The only reliable source is that of experience either on the part of the individual or that of the group to which one belongs.

The criterion to be followed is that of gaining pleasure and happiness and avoiding pain. It is not the pleasure of the movement that is important, nor is it proper to disregard the happiness of others. One must consider all long-range consequences that are associated with one's acts and, in light of these, choose those actions or make those decisions which will make life more pleasant and happy.

Classes of Hedonism

Patterson[28] has pointed out the generality of the term *pleasure* and indicates that hedonistic theories may be classified into particular types depending upon the kind of pleasure that is accepted as the norm or standard of goodness. For example, he differentiates the pleasure base by saying that it makes a difference whether the pleasure refers to one's own or the pleasure of others, to pleasures of the moment or to life as a whole, whether pleasure might be sensuous or intellectual or aesthetic, whether it may motivate us to action without choice or to which we voluntarily respond. For these reasons, Patterson presents the following classifications of hedonism:

1. *Psychological hedonism.* This is the doctrine that all people do pursue their own pleasure. It is based on the psychological analysis of people's motives which cause them to act as they do. It takes the view that people are selfish and work only for their pleasurable interests. They may try to disguise their actions so as to appear altruistic and noble, but the psychological hedonist knows differently and sees behind these pretentions.

   For example, consider the teacher who performs research and publishes, not for the contribution it may make to furthering knowledges, but to enhance salary and promotion purposes; or the parent who forces the child at eight or ten years of age into an emotionally administered athletic program under the motive of contributing to the future ability and welfare of the child, but in reality to satisfy the parent's own ego; or the sports coach who competitively recruits the superior performer with altruistically phrased reasons, but really to enhance the coach's own image, prestige, and financial status.

   The doctrine of psychological hedonism is claimed to be an unproven assumption. There may be motives other than one's personal pleasure, or one may not at all be aware of pleasure seeking when performing actions.

2. *Ethical hedonism.* This is the doctrine that people *ought* to pursue pleasure. The ethical hedonist claims that it is a mistake for one not to pursue pleasure above all other choices because pleasure is the one and only ultimate good, and therefore it is a waste to spend time and effort

towards any other end. This doctrine supports the decision that when choices of amounts of pleasure are possible, one should always choose the alternative that promises the greatest amount of pleasure. The choice can be assisted by enlisting past experience and the judgment of others.

The doctrine of ethical hedonism has met with some difficulties in acceptance, particularly the criticism shown as the *hedonistic paradox*. It is often the pursuit of a goal that brings happiness to people, not the actual attainment of it. Happiness may result from the activity engaged in the process rather than from achieving the product.

3. *Individualistic hedonism.* This doctrine holds that persons, in order to pursue the good life, must pursue their *own* pleasure. This doctrine places the individual into the number one position in the priorities of life. One should not work for the sake of the pleasure or welfare of others except as such efforts are advantageous to oneself.

For example, the pleasure and satisfaction that the highly skilled sports performer receives as a result of success should be placed in the first position of all values, even to the extent of using other team members to achieve such personal pleasures. The welfare of the team or its members is only second in importance. The individual does not compete or sacrifice for the welfare of the team, but only for his or her own pleasure and self-aggrandizement.

4. *Universalistic hedonism.* This doctrine holds that the ultimate standard of goodness is the greatest amount of happiness for the greatest number of persons. It advocates the happiness of all people and for all time insofar as this goal is possible of attainment, even though this goal might be in conflict with one's own pleasure.

Since our primary interest insofar as physical education and sport exists in relation to the ethical theory of pleasure, and happiness lies in the theory of utilitarianism, we shall look more closely at the substance of this theory.

Distinctive Features of Utilitarianism

Probably the best known contribution that English thought has made to moral philosophy was that of Jeremy Bentham, James Mill, and John Stuart Mill. Utilitarianism had its greatest reception from the middle of the eighteenth to the middle of the nineteenth century. It was a time of heightened industrialization, of intolerable class and working conditions for the masses, and of challenge to the existing economic and political structures. Utilitarianism represented an essentially democratic moral theory: All persons are entitled to the good things of life; each person is counted as a person in any moral consideration; there is to be no discrimination because of sex, color, economic class, or social or political status.

As we examine the concept of utilitarianism, we might note its distinctive features that serve as a basis for principles upon which one might draw for guidance in ethical actions or decisions:

1. The starting point of utilitarianism is that the experience of pleasure alone is to be considered intrinsically good and desirable for its own sake. Anything that is good in any other sense must be a means to the achievement of pleasure.

2. The general object or aim of life is the maximization of pleasure, and this is identified with the achievement of the greatest amount of happiness.

3. The determination of the rightness of any action undertaken by an individual is to be judged by its consequences in terms of leading to a happier life for others. This feature serves as a base for the answer to the question, What should be our aim in life? It stresses an evaluation of the consequences in order to select the one which promises the greatest happiness for the person or, if more than one person is involved, for the greatest number.

4. The extent to which our political and social institutions and even our man-made laws are to be judged is on the basis of the extent to which they minister to the welfare and happiness of persons affected by those institutions

and laws. The ultimate question to be asked is, How effective are institutions and laws or codes which touch the lives of persons in producing a more satisfactory and happier life for those persons who live under the sanctions or policies of such institutions or laws? This question implies the only relevant moral consideration in determining the worth of our political, educational, and other social institutions created for the service of people. John Dewey aptly described it when he said, "Utilitarianism subordinated law to human achievement instead of subordinating humanity to eternal law. Institutions are made for man and not man for institutions" (p. 180).

Dewey's statement and its meanings have often been applied to the context of sport by stating, "Sport was made for man and not man for sport."

5. The intent of utilitarianism is universalistic in nature. It is not egoistic or selfish as are some types of hedonism and humanism, nor is its application to be made only to a small group of privileged people or specifically designated groups, such as the affluent, the professions, those in power, athletes, the cultured, or those with special identification.

The Theories of Jeremy Bentham

Jeremy Bentham (1748-1832) proposed a system of ethics that would be independent of theology and yet provide direction for correcting those conditions which interfered with the proper development of society. He also proposed a method for dealing with ethical problems that would provide some type of assurance and accuracy as methods used in the physical sciences. His *An Introduction To The Principles Of Morals And Legislation*[3] contains the statement, "Nature has placed mankind under the governance of two sovereign masters, pain and pleasure. It is for them alone to point out what we ought to do, as well as to determine what we shall do" (p. 11).

Bentham, in support of the basic principles of psychological and ethical hedonism, believed that pleasure or its expectation is the primary motive of why persons perform as they do and dominates the course of life. *How* the person seeks to obtain happiness constitutes the moral problem. If it is sought contrary to the happiness of other persons, actions are not good. It is by working for the happiness of other people that an individual finds one's own happiness and thus achieves the only life that can be called good. The principle that Bentham supported is that the essential element in moral conduct is the action on the part of the person to increase the amount of happiness which may be experienced by members of the whole society.

It is true that Bentham sought to distinguish between which pleasures are better than others. This effort led to the construction of his "calculus of pleasures," a device which would enable one to measure the values of conflicting pleasures. Since the device recognized only quantitative distinctions, considerable controversy exists as to its comprehensiveness in the value of its use.

Bentham, in stating that one's private interests in seeking happiness also contributed to the public welfare, recognized that there would be short-sighted and malevolent persons who would seek ends not beneficial to themselves or to society.

For example, it may be true that one cannot consistently circumvent the rules of the game in an attempt to win, but there may be those who think they can, and hence we have serious moral violators. It may be true that honesty and sportsmanlike conduct is the best policy, but there are some to whom winning the contest is the only thing, and so we have dishonesty in sport. The question that arises is, How can people be prevented from pursuing their apparent selfish interests which may be harmful to the welfare of the group or the public?

Bentham presented an answer to this question by proposing that sanctions (coercive intervention to the violation of a law) be applied. Since there are those who are short-sighted, imprudent, or ignorant, it is necessary that pain (punishment) be applied to a point where such persons behave in a manner which conforms to the public interest.

Sanctions are of four types: *physical*, which would be the

natural pains that follow the performance of an unethical act; *political*, which would be the pains added to certain acts by those appointed to administer justice (such as the loss of privileges, probation, detention, loss of post-season or TV programs); *moral*, or pains that are the result of spontaneous reactions of members of the group or community (such as disapproval); and *religious*, or those pains which come from the hand of a superior, invisible being either in this life or the life to come.

The Theories of John Stuart Mill

John Stuart Mill (1806-1873), in his essay entitled *Utilitarianism*, introduced modifications of Bentham's doctrines by adding qualitative distinctions in deciding which pleasures are better than others, an argument that continues among critics. For our purposes, we are to note that Mill attempted to bind together the egoistic doctrine of psychological hedonism and the altruistic doctrine of the principle of utility with the addition of the internal sanction of conscience to Bentham's previously named four sanctions.

The Principle of Utility

Mill's principle of utility holds that we ought to pursue the greatest happiness of the greatest number. The principle of utility expresses a system of morals. It advances the law which defines the difference between right and wrong. The belief in this *greatest happiness* principle holds that actions are right as they tend to promote happiness, or wrong if they tend to promote the reverse of happiness. Mill believed everything that is desired is desired either as a means of happiness or as a part of happiness itself. The utilitarian system has its foundation in human nature, that is, in people's desire for personal happiness, in their desire to be in unity with their fellow creatures, and in their feeling of sympathy. These human interests can find fulfillment in a society based on the principle of utility. Thus, utilitarian ethics is essential for any social order so as to win the support and cooperation of people who are free and equal.

This concept of the relations between the individual and one's fellow humans is based on the recognition between equals and on the understanding that the interests of all are to be regarded equally. Since everyone's interest is in one's own happiness, the only workable moral rules in a free society, a society of equals, are rules designed to promote the greatest happiness for the greatest number.

The Internal Sanction of Conscience

Again, as with the doctrines of Bentham, the question arises, How can people be persuaded always to act in accord with the utility principle? How can people be persuaded or forced to pursue the happiness of others since Mill has stated that the ultimate motive for human action is the pursuit of private happiness?

In addition to Bentham's four sanctions, Mill adds a fifth as the ultimate sanction for the principle of utility. This is the *internal sanction of conscience.* Conscience as a feeling in one's own mind is connected with the idea of duty; one feels pain when duty or a standard of right is violated. This feeling can be cultivated by social conditioning and education. This sanction seems to naturally connect with the utility principle because of natural feelings of human unity and sympathy. All forces which bear upon the growth of the individual, such as education and its components — teachers, administrators, coaches, and others — should cultivate the feeling of conscience associated with the principle of utility.

Expectations that the internal sanction of conscience is operable in physical education and sport situations raises many basic questions. These questions relate not alone to the structure and function of human nature but to the environmental forces which act upon the human organism so as to cause it to respond as it does. One may ask, for example, Who are likely to be the winners in the highly competitive climate of sport where winning is the primary goal? If one seeks the confidence, respect, and good will of one's fellow humans as a means of achieving happiness in life, how can the actions of honesty, generosity, and working in the interest of others' welfare or the welfare of society be reconciled with the intent to achieve superiority in defeating one's opponent? Might it be true that the good guys always finish last? There has long been a question as to whether or not the *good guy*, characterized by the one who demonstrates consideration for others, sportsmanship, and effort to perform in the spirit as well as the letter of the rules, can survive in a highly competitive environment.

Whether or not conscience can be used as a sanction against the occurrence of these human qualities thought to be inimical to those which physical education and sport declare to be within their domain of teaching, education, and training has and continues to remain questionable. The use of conscience as a deterrent to unethical actions in sport will depend, in large measure, not solely on the high quality of educational leadership, but also on the development of high standards of ethical behavior at all levels in the educational process.

IV. THE COMPETITIVE STRUGGLE FOR POWER

Those who wish to embrace the ethical theories of hedonism and, principally, utilitarianism — which supports the concept that goodness is found in the greatest happiness for the greatest number of persons — will find no consolation or enthusiasm for the theories of the naturalists. This will be particularly so as the contrast pertains to the theories of Friedrich Nietzsche which we shall examine.

Ethical theories which pertain to the competitive struggle for power have been developed over the centuries by a number of thinkers and in a variety of ways. Collectively they have sought the answers to the meaning of moral life in (1) the struggle for survival related to biological evolution and its processes, (2) the search for security by persons haunted by fear of their fellow humans, (3) the power struggle of politics, and (4) the aggressive competition for wealth and power in the many areas of economic life.

It would seem reasonable and appropriate to add a fifth category for application of this group of ethical theories, namely, the competitive struggle to achieve superiority in recognition, prestige, power, and status through winning in competitive sport. To varying degrees, the motive for struggle are found in all categories — survival, security, power, and economic gain.

The Doctrine of Naturalism

Naturalism is concerned with the way humans actually behave, and its adherents are convinced that nature is the only source from which standards of morality can be derived. By accepting nature, rather than individual feelings, they place ethics on a scientific basis so that its conclusions can be established as are those in the sciences. They are skeptical about any standard that has never been realized in human experience. They are not to be influenced by personal desires but are guided by actual observed facts.

The naturalists identify a basic principle that resides in all human behavior, that is, a form of self-interest as the dominant motive in each person. Therefore, all human beings are regarded as selfish, each seeking the fulfillment of his or her own nature and thus acting in competition with everyone else. Since individual interests clash with one another, they cannot all reach their goal. Some are going to lose out, and their welfare will be sacrificed in order that others may gain their ends. Not everyone can win. The expectation is, of course, that those who are stronger than their competitors will achieve the good things of life, while the losers, weaker ones, will have to get along as best they can. It is this phase of the naturalistic doctrine that finds its expression in the phrase, "might makes right."

Application to Plants and Animals

A demonstration of this principle is found in nature and is recognized as a universal law. If one examines the processes of life among plants and animals in nature, a person will find many examples of the operation of this principle of naturalistic ethics. It condemns meekness, humility, generosity, and self-sacrifice, while it glorifies aggression, cruelty, and exploitation. For example, plants must compete with each other for sustenance when available space and food supplies are low. Survival of the strong will consist of crowding out and thus destroying the lives of others. Trees which attempt to grow in limited sunlight will struggle to reach heights necessary for the light, while weaker ones which cannot make it will die. All beasts in the wild look out for themselves and do not hesitate to take advantage of others where survival is at stake; it is the only method to employ. It is as though nature tells them, "If you are not strong and ruthless in dealing with your opponents you cannot continue to live." Cooperative relationships in survival matters are undertaken only to preserve the existence of oneself or loved ones. This process might illustrate the principle of *natural selection* whereby the strong continue to exist by crushing the weak. It also illustrates the concept of *survival of the fittest.*

Application to Humans

The naturalist contends that this principle of self-interest, being a universal law of nature, also applies to human beings. Regardless of how altruistic or unselfish persons may claim to be, their actions are ultimately tied to their own selfish interests, be it for power, money, glory, or whatever. Illustrations of the application of this view can be seen in many categories of vocations and professions. It can be seen in politics, where politicians are to work in behalf of the interests of the public rather than for private interests. It can be seen in athletics, where the motives include the development of winning records which enhance the personal prestige and economic status of the coach. The naturalists are not fooled by exterior show. They know that, rather than loyalty to the common good of humans, as well as all other creatures in nature, people are governed by the principle of self-interest. This, in turn, makes their existence and survival possible, depending upon the standards which they establish for themselves.

The Doctrine of Machiavelli

Niccolo Machiavelli (1469-1527) advanced a doctrine for rulers in government which was tested only in the practical results achieved. If kindness, truthfulness, and honesty are effective in getting what one wants, it is proper to employ these. But if a more effective means involves deceit, cruelty, or injustice, the strong should use these. After all, *the end justifies the means*. It is more important to seem virtuous than to be virtuous. It is not what you really are that counts in success, but what people think you are. Those in power have no obligation to be truthful and honest in dealing with their constituents. A successful ruler will employ both cunning and power, and if one fails, the other can be relied upon.

The Doctrines of Darwin and Spencer

Charles Darwin (1809-1892) and Herbert Spencer (1820-1903) contributed importantly to naturalistic ethics. While both have been associated with the theory of evolution, a brief presentation of the essential elements in the contribution to ethics from each will be helpful. While Darwin's work was in the field of biological science, Spencer saw in the theory of evolution its implication for the social and moral experiences of all people.

Darwin, in the main, proposed the principle of *natural selection,* or that individuals or species survive in accordance with their ability to adapt themselves to their environment. Since all compete for a place in the environment (according to one's needs and ends), only those who possess the strength or the ingenuity to beat out their competitors will succeed in achieving their place. The losers will have to vie for themselves or die off. It will thus be a struggle for existence and a survival of the fittest. Darwin did advance four points which are of particular interest. These are that (1) no two members of any species are exactly alike, but there is a proven variation among them; (2) there is an on-going struggle for existence in one's environment, but chiefly for food and against disease and predatory enemies; (3) organisms which are stronger and adapt better to their environments because they are stronger will win over their competitors in the struggle for existence; (4) parents will transmit their own characteristics to their offspring through physical and biological means of heredity.

Spencer's philosophy of evolution is most appropriate in its application to ethics. He popularized the doctrine of evolution and placed his ethical theories on a scientific base. For example, Spencer declared that ethical principles should not be derived for some authoritarian nor intuitive source but should be examined by the methods of science and brought into agreement by observed facts. Their validity would be tested, as in any other field of knowledge. The task of the student of ethics is to discover how ideas of right and wrong have evolved from human experiences, which is the primary source of data for ethics.

Spencer, then, declared those activities are good which organisms (including humans) have engaged in and which, through their experiences, they have found to enable them to survive. Those activities which cause destruction of life or are contrary to physical well-being are bad. It is through the striving for a better adaptation to one's environment that persons achieve peace and happiness. If nature is permitted to proceed in its own way, the weak and inferior will be eliminated. Then the strong will produce strong succeeding generations of the species. The weak and inefficient should not be protected from exploitation by the strong, for then, the weak will continue to produce inferior offspring. Society itself will become weakened if one interferes with nature. Government should take no measures to help those who need help. Assistance through such programs as food stamps, social security, medicaid and medicare, regulation of prices, old age assistance, etc., should be abandoned, because these measures represent interference with nature taking its own direction.

The application of Spencer's doctrine to physical education and sport finds some variance as to effect. The doctrine would seem to be contrary in principle and practice to the basic beliefs upheld by a democratic society which gives support to the worth of the human personality. We might observe two instances in physical education and sport where the doctrine is refuted and supported, respectively.

Observe, on the one hand, the establishment of national, state, and local organizations to seek a harmonious answer to problems which arise from the unequalization of conditions under which competitive sport might function. The experience of attempting to seek an administration of sensible and equitable programs of competitive sport has resulted in the establishment of classifications of divisions, classes, conferences, and leagues of teams and individual performers. These structures bring together those who possess like philosophies, principles, and policies. Their functional relationships are based upon an equalization of conditions and abilities so as to prevent exploitation of the weak by the strong, an occurrence which would likely result in the elimination of the vast majority of intercollegiate and interscholastic sport teams.

Observe, on the other hand, the methods applied by some who, in adapting to their environment, employ the Spencerian theory: the neglectful teaching of large numbers of students of physical education classes by the so-called ball tosser, the teacher-coach, in order to devote teaching time to other matters pertaining to the sport team or up-coming game; or the assignment of students in the physical education class to the bleachers or study hall while the teacher-coach works with members of the sport team; or the football coach who schedules an early season intensive scrimmage to weed out those who shouldn't survive and identify those who should.

In all such instances, the primary motive is one of survival in an environment where the pressures to meet public expectations demand winning performances. Means are found to adapt to the environment which employ methods that enhance survival.

Appeal of the Doctrine of Naturalism

Before proceeding to Nietzsche's theories involving the competitive struggle for power, we need to ask the question, Why has the doctrine of naturalism in ethics received rather widespread attention and often approval? There are two primary reasons for its reception. One is its claim to adherence to scientific method, a procedure not always applied in the field of ethics. The naturalist draws conclusions based on observed facts of human behavior and builds on a solid empirical base. The naturalist does not make presumptions of the existence of an absolute goodness nor an imaginary ideal which has never been observed in actuality. The actual observance of the processes of nature in action lends itself ideally to take such a stand. It is relatively easy for people to understand the naturalists' conclusions because their own experiences of observation may be identical.

Second, the naturalist is able to create in others a feeling of rapport, of receptiveness to explanations of the theory because of openness and candor. There results a mutual sharing of recognition of human experiences based on the selfishness of mankind. One doesn't feel deceived by being taken through a maze of logic in justification of rather vague relationships as sometimes exists in the presentation of ethical theory. It is all there, and it is highly realistic in terms of personal experiences.

Some of the most realistic examples of the acknowledgement and acceptance of the naturalistic philosophy are found in competitive sport at all levels — professional, college, school, or under community auspices. The platitude, "It is not whether you win or lose, it is how you play the game," has no relevancy in the context of naturalism. One either wins, or one loses. There is no question concerning the criterion for success whether applied to the team, individual, or coach.

Nietzsche's Struggle for Power Theory

The writings of Friedrich Nietzsche (1844-1900)[26] represent an extreme ethical view from that taken by Christianity or those found in the ideals of a democratic philosophy. Yet his reflections on the subject of ethical conduct have created an influence on the life and thinking of those in nations throughout the world. He did not base his theories on observed facts and on a rational mind, as did Darwin and Spencer, but instead on an energy, a power, a striving in human nature or, in essence, in a *will to power*. He says, "A living thing seeks above all to *discharge* its strength; life itself is *Will to Power*; self-preservation is only one of the indirect and most frequent results thereof" (p. 116).

Will to Power is instinctive in all living forms. Forms which live contrary to this Will are degenerate, and when people permit themselves to become conditioned by religion and philosophies so as to define life, they lose their true identities. This Will to Power explains why living creatures struggle. If persons have no goal they have nothing on which to focus their Will. The only good to strive for in a higher stage of evolution is that of Superman.

Since there is no higher good to which the Will to Power is subordinate, persons should use any means they have to acquire more of it. One may use deceit, cruelty, and violence if it seems appropriate. Exploitation and deception will be practiced by those in whom the will to power is achieving its highest expression. In the competition or struggle for power, the winners will become the masters, the losers will become slaves. This master and slave morality recognizes that persons will belong to different ranks and will not be equal. The greatest point of contrast in the master morality versus the slave morality is that masters will be harsh, selfish, and aggressive. Terms such as noble, courtly, frank, gentlemanly, and chivalrous will benefit the character of the master class. The lower classes will lie and cringe, and terms such as villainous, scurrilous, knavish, slavish, vulgar, mercenary, and so forth, will denote them. Feeling a superabundance of power, the noble type is generous to the weak only because it proves superiority and an opportunity to discharge strength.

Here we have a doctrine which proclaims a different set of rules or moral principles for each of the separate classes and not one set binding on all people. The masters simply use their power to subjugate the masses and use them as a means to realize their own ambitions.

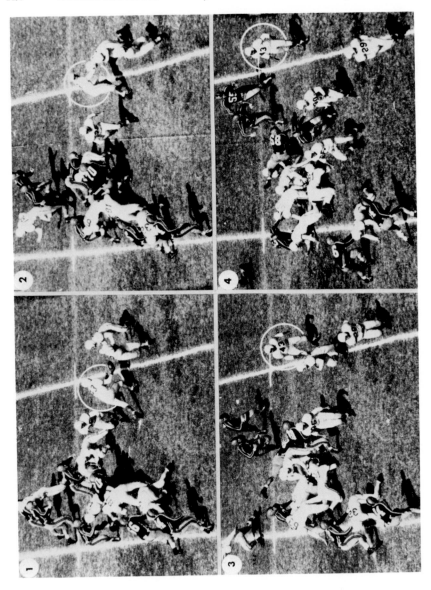

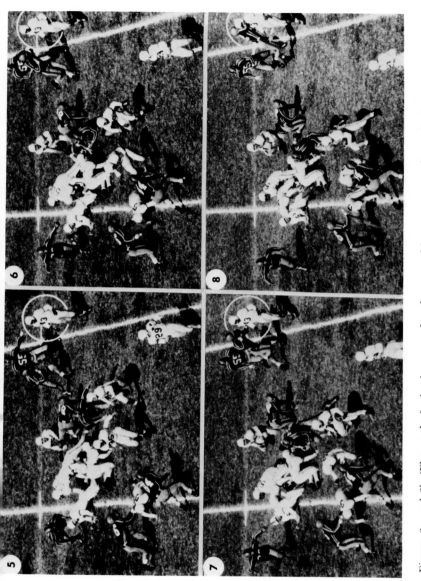

Figure 6a and 6b. The goal of winning can often become of importance to the exclusion of all other values. The doctrine of naturalism and the Nietzsche theory support the practice of might makes right. Courtesy, Des Moines Register-Tribune.

Thus we have the production of supermen and superwomen who rise above the masses and have no empathy for them. We also see that Nietzsche's theory bitterly opposes conventional morality and democracy. The democratic ideal of holding the individual person as of infinite worth and as the end for which all else exists is anathema to Nietzsche. He particularly condemned the influence of Judeo-Christian ideals in our Western tradition as the basis of conventional morality. The ethical teachings of Christianity are appropriate for slaves. The democratic devotion to the welfare of the common person was the antithesis to Nietzsche's true morality. His *true* morality would make a *transvaluation of values* that would substitute a leadership of *supermen,* i.e. *free and noble spirits,* for the Judeo-Christian traditions and who would create their own values. The good and productive in human culture would be provided by the strong, assertive, and aristocratic. The weak and oppressed, *the bungled and botched* would cling together for self-protection against the strong and powerful.

Nietzsche's theory, while representing an extreme view, is not unknown in its application to all types of areas of human endeavor, including physical education and sport. This is because Nietzsche recognized the existence of the will to power in the very nature of some persons. The drive for the elements of power and prestige which may accompany higher level administrative positions in physical education and sport has been and can be evidenced. The application of deceit and exploitation through personal and political means to realize one's own ambition for power is not an uncommon technique.

The intensive drive by coaches of sport to achieve the objective of being number one through the unethical use of persons as a means in the process is documented. The deviation from established and approved rules in order to achieve championship status is often cited.

V. THE INDIVIDUAL AND SELF-REALIZATION AS THE SEAT OF VALUE

The ethics of self-realization and their supporting concepts will find a wide appeal from among teachers of physical education and teachers and coaches of sport. There is a natural relation between the concepts which underlie the ideals, motives, and desires of those who spend a large amount of their lives in the field of education, devoting their time and energies toward assisting others to develop their individual capacities and potantialities, and the concepts of goodness and rightness of the self-realizationists. A presentation of the primary essentials of the ethics of self-realization will help to clarify this relationship.

The standard of what is good and right in the ethics of self-realization is the fulfillment or realization of the capacities and potentialities which are present in the human nature of each person. This standard is a prominent, representative one which appears in the goals of education. It is implicitly recognized as an outcome of the application of a code of ethics among personnel in educational organizations. It is also represented in the foundation principles which underlie the functioning of a democratic society which views the individual person as the end for which all else exists.

Self-realization may be identified as a teleological theory of ethics (one which accepts as the standard of goodness some particular end or goal toward which actions are directed). It finds the standard of goodness in the harmonious development of all components included in the human personality and/or the maximum fulfillment of the capacities and potentialities that are present in all human beings. Actions are considered to be morally good only when they contribute toward those ends.

Self-realization represents a doctrine that has found expression in the ethical teachings of Confucius, in the philosophies of the Greek teachers Plato and Aristotle, in the literature of the Old Testament, in the moral ideas of Christianity, and in the ethical writings of some of the prominent philosophers of the western world. Because of the variations in interpretations of self-realization ethics, one must view each expression in the context of a writer's production. Some of the most prominent of these will be found among the listed references in the text bibliography.

The Role of the Self

An understanding of the ethics of self-realization requires an examination of the role of the self since it is toward the self that all good actions are directed. Several points related to the self which need to be presented are as follows:

1. One must think of the concept of the total self as an ideal one, that is, one whose total capacities are developed in a harmonious manner rather than what might occur to any one capacity at any particular moment. Since this concept represents an ideal, it may never be realized. It does represent a base from which a person can relate one's thinking relative to the total self. The educational process, if it is to constitute an important factor in assisting the self to become fully realized, takes considerable time planned in accordance to a definite pattern. The self in this concept represents the final product of the forces of education working on the individual so as to develop as ideally as possible the kind of self that would exist if its best potentialities were to be realized. Since the capacities of persons differ, each has an individuality to achieve and a uniqueness to attain.

2. If one were to consider all questions which relate to the nature of the self, many would relate to endless controversies and could not be answered with finality. There are some facts, however, pertaining to the existence of self and human nature, which are listed as follows: (a) The self does possess a body. The physical educator will have no problem identifying with this fact. The body is an instrument for the expression of personality; it can be somatotyped; its physiological components are susceptible to change with work or exercise; and the components which comprise motor skills are related to skill efficiency. (b) The self does possess a mind. The mind, in its conscious state, is capable of bringing meaning to events and things to which it is exposed, of bringing into a conscious and comprehensive unity nontemporal events and abstractions. (c) The self possesses a basic quality of wanting, of desiring, of striving for things in life which are mean-

ingful to it for the sake of realizing its own ends as it sees them. The self possesses desires for the possession of material objects and, in the process of striving to achieve them, contributes to self-realization. The self desires friends and comradeship or a sense of personal relationships. It includes relatives, friends, associates, and others who are part of the self's consciousness. (d) The self has a natural tendency to acquire knowledge of life and the world about it, all of which contributes to self-realization through the enlargement and enrichment of the perspective of life and the scope of selfhood. (e) The self possesses an unrelenting pursuit of ideals. The self is constantly looking for new horizons, of better ways of living, of conquering new fields, of achieving and seeking recognition, of helping humankind. Only by doing so can the self fulfill an essential part of its nature as a human being. It pushes toward new frontiers because of discontent with present status or a curiosity of what lies beyond. Why does one climb Mt. Everest? "Because it is there." The conquest represents the fulfillment of an ideal, a challenge which lies within the heart and mind of self who achieves in them. Its achievement or failure is personal and thus a part of one's true self.

3. It is not to be expected that perfection of an ideal type of person is to be achieved. Modern interpretations of the theory see self-realization for each person consisting in the achievement of one's own perfection, in all that makes for a full and abundant life and included in the good for the person. But no two people have the same capacities, and everyone has his or her own individuality to achieve and a uniqueness to attain. In this sense, self-realization constitutes a much more substantial standard for goodness and right than other theories contain.

There is a recognized difficulty that arises out of any concept of maximum realization of all one's components that comprise self. Often, persons are subject to many of the influences of the human and physical environment that surrounds them. Much depends on the times in which one lives, the individually uncontrollable conditions in which one resides, and the role one assumes in vocations and professions. Persons are always placed into positions where choices must be made and rejections effected. This view supports the contention that it is impossible to realize *all* one's potential self; if we are to realize our best possible self, then guidance is needed. William James[14] recognized this difficulty:

> With most objects of desire, physical nature restricts our choice to but one of many represented goods, and even so it is here. I am often confronted with the necessity of standing by one of my empirical selves and relinquishing the best. Not that I would not, if I could be both handsome and fat and well-dressed, and a great athlete, and make a million a year, be a wit, a *bon-vivant,* and a lady-killer, as well as a philosopher, a philanthropist, statesman, warrior, and African explorer, as well as a *love-poet* and saint. But the thing is simply impossible. The millionaire's work would run counter to the saint's; *bon-vivant* and the philanthropist would trip each other up; the philosopher and the lady-killer could not well keep house in the same tenement of clay. Such different characters may conceivably at the outset of life be alike *possible.* But to make any one of them actual, the rest must be more or less suppressed. (Pp. 209-210)

4. It would be a mistake to think of the components of the self or the facts that comprise its nature as existing in isolation one from the other. The self is more than any one and more than the sum of all of these. The ideal of self-realization is a complete integration of all the elements that make up one's total personality and nature through loyalty to an ideal that brings one into complete harmony with the ultimate source of value in terms of goodness and right. Self is a unity which represents the integration of all its parts into a single, harmoniously functioning whole.

How Best to Achieve Integration of Self

How is this state of integration for the full realization of self to be achieved? How, in the process of striving to achieve the development of self, can conflicts between the recognized components be avoided? Isn't it of too great expectation for all of them to be realized or fulfilled?

Integration can be accomplished best by identifying and selecting a certain end as a goal to be achieved in preference to others. It requires the organization of one's goals in priority order with a recognition of the most important values in one's life. Lesser goals or interests must be subordinated and satisfied only as they contribute to the process of achieving the larger goal and are in harmony with the process. *Thus, one selects the dominant goal or purpose, organizes the priority of activities, and subordinates the lesser goals to the achievement of the greater goal, contributing and harmonizing with it.* Conflicts which may arise as a result of attempting to spread oneself too much in the desire to seek self-realization in all component areas are better resolved.

The complete integration of all components which comprise the total self is an ideal only. No human being achieves all components to his or her fullest capacity or potentiality. Human life experiences and the short span of human life represent limiting factors. As with all principles, however, the failure to achieve them does not in any way invalidate the principles. It is best to think of progress in terms of the *degree* to which one more closely achieves the ideal.

The organization of goal planning which recognizes the dominant goal as a means toward self development in no way ignores the attempt to achieve subordinate goals. It simply concentrates attention and effort upon the central goal but looks to the realization of other concomitants in the process.

This is a process well recognized and utilized by the physical educator and coach of sports. While the process of training the physical body and the development of physical skills for more efficient performances may constitute the primary objective of the student, he or she also achieves, if the proper conditions exist, other important goals. These would include the realization of mental processes, high standards of social behavior, increase of social relationships, the successful pursuit of ideals established by the self, and above all an integration of the personality through striving toward the accomplishment of dominant goals.

A Standard of Goodness for Self-Realization

Before leaving the presentation of the main features of what is a representative view of the theory of self-realization, it is important to note that a major problem in ethical theory is related to the question concerning the existence of a valid norm or standard in accordance with which human conduct can be judged as good or bad.

Patterson[28] holds that for self-realization,

> The norm or standard of goodness for the ethical realist is the complete realization of selfhood. This can be accomplished only through a process of organization and integration of the various elements that are involved. One's real self must always be identified with the ideal self. The ideal self is one in which all the parts are related organically to the whole so that each separate activity finds its meaning in relation to the whole and the whole self is something that finds expression in and through each of its parts. Furthermore, the selfhood of any particular individual must be related organically to a goal or purpose which includes the development and realization of every other finite self. In this way the ultimate goal of the universe, or, in other words, the purpose of the infinite self is achieved through the fulfillment of the best possibilities that are latent in each individual. (p. 292)

Many contemporary philosophers have had a tendency to withdraw support from this theory because of its metaphysical base (a theory which takes a view of the nature of existence and a person's place in it). The influence of empiricism (a practice of relying on experience or observation alone rather than upon a rationalistic means in the pursuit of knowledge) has caused a revision in the thinking of modern day thinkers who seem to have lost faith in any kind of a system based on metaphysics. However, there are those who do maintain a spiritual interpretation of reality and utilize this support in the teaching of ethics. Some of the most prominent of these are Thomas H. Green, Francis H. Bradley, and Josiah Royce, whose sources of information are listed in the bibliography.

Finally, as has been pointed out, the full realization of all the values associated with the ideal of development of the characteristics in human nature represents an ideal only. The complete achievement is limited by the experiences of human existence and of lack of time. But this does not mean an abandonment of the ideal. The ideal should serve as an end or goal toward which activities can be directed. What is needed for a closer approximation of the achievement of the ideal of self-realization is an organization of values in an effort to overcome conflicts between the various elements which exist in human nature. To do this the values of human life must be arranged in some sort of order.

An Organization of Values

Patterson[28] presents three principles to determine the ordering of values to best achieve the ideal of self-realization. These are as follows: (1) Intrinsic values are more important than instrumental or extrinsic ones. This means that values such as money and power are valuable only as a *means* for realizing spiritual ends, or that physical development and well-being or play, recreation, and competitive sports, while somewhat intrinsic in value, are really instrumental in achieving larger ends expressed in spiritual good. (2) Permanent values should be rated higher than transient ones. This means that experiences which relate to the ideals or spirit of a person are more important than those which arise from the senses or that are sensual. Spiritual values are more permanent. (3) Values which are productive of more values are of a higher order than those which are not productive. For example, one should share with others those things which enrich another's life, which in turn enriches his or her own life. This is especially so with such values of an aesthetic, spiritual, humanitarian, or intellectual type.

Figure 7. The ideal of self-realization is a complete integration of all the elements that make up one's total personality through loyalty to an ideal that brings one into complete harmony with the ultimate source of value in terms of goodness and right. Self is a unity which represents the integration of all its parts into a single, harmoniously functioning whole.

The goal, then, lies in the culturing of those factors which contribute to the development of the human person and in the perfection of his or her functions. It embraces the humanistic concept that human beings as persons exist as *ends* in themselves and never as *means* only.

DISCUSSION TOPICS AND ETHICAL INCIDENTS

1. In what ways may a study of ethical theories assist one to better clarify an issue, to find one's own basic answers to ethical problems, to comprise one's own ethical concepts and ideals? For example, illustrate how you might apply ethical theory to the question of whether or not coaches of sports should be evaluated in terms of educational goals rather than the commercial objectives of wins and losses, money taken at the gate, or publicity and notoriety afforded to teams and institutions. (pp. 78-80.)

2. Explain the nature of ethical relativism in terms of athletes who, in opposition to authoritarian and disciplinary types of coaches, wish to exert their personal freedoms related to life styles and appearance. What are the factors which have been responsible for the shift in attitudes toward life and interpersonal relations with their emphasis on human rights and human values? (pp. 83, 86.)

3. Based upon your own experiences, how would you classify physical education teachers and athletic coaches in relation to being absolutists or relativists? Compare your experience and classifications with other members of the class. (p. 86.)

4. The high school physical education teacher opens an office and small gymnasium at home and publicly advertises a program of service to the public for remunerative purposes. The program, offered evenings, is intended for adults who are interested in figure control, weight reduction, and physical fitness. Other teachers, including those in physical education, condemn the action as being unprofessional. On which of the three levels of ethical relativism (emotive, egoistic, and cultural) does this action of the peer group exist? (pp. 87-89.)

5. Would an authoritarian or democratic type of management

(coaching, etc.) be more effective in the development of a successfully functioning athletic team whose primary goal is winning? Compare the basic elements contained in both types of social structures before arriving at your decision. Is it possible that the number one college team in the country in the so-called major sport category is capable of reconciling the differences between the authoritarian and democratic approach to coaching? (pp. 89-90.)

6. In accordance with Kant's moral law or Categorical Imperative, either the rules that govern the administration of sports and the conduct of sports and games are to be fully supported or there will be no rules at all. How do you account for the inconsistency in the adherence to established rules by some individuals, and yet the continued existence of athletic programs? (pp. 101-102.)

7. Suppose that all of the rules which govern the actual playing of games were eliminated. What would you expect to be the behavior of the participants in any single contest, particularly if the contest was a physical contact sport? Would your answer to the question cause you to wonder whether or not the conduct of participants in sport represents outward conformity to rules but not necessarily in the context of a rational will? Keep in mind that Kant emphasized that actions have moral worth only if they are the products of a rational will. Do participants adhere to the rules of the games because of sanctions or penalties if the rules are broken or because of a conviction of moral worth? (p. 102.)

8. Sport, according to the ethical theory on the pursuit of happiness as a basic human right, is to be judged on the basis to which it ministers to the needs, welfare, and happiness of those who participate in it. John Dewey's statement that institutions were made for man and not man for institutions has often been modified to indicate that sport as an institution was made for man and not man for sport. How does this concept contained in this ethical theory compare with the concept that winning is the only thing? (p. 108.)

9. The naturalist (competitive struggle for power) is no dreamer or idealist devoted to absolute goodness when it comes

to acting in competition with others. Winning is the *only* thing to the naturalist, whether the goal be survival, money, power, or glory. The results of contests as recorded on the sports pages are realistic and represent the basis upon which judgments of success or failure are made. Is Nietzsche's struggle for power theory evidenced at some levels of competition and among some persons in the field of sport? List some examples of practices used by coaches of sports teams which are intended to enhance personal survival in an environment where winning is expected. (pp. 113, 122.)

10. The complete integration of all the elements that make up one's total personality might be achieved through loyalty to an ideal and persistent pursuit of that ideal. Explain how one may select as the dominant goal in life the following sequence of life-time events: making the team, becoming a successful sports performer, and devoting one's life to teaching and coaching in physical education and sport. What might be some of the subordinate goals that contribute to and harmonize with this dominant goal of life? (pp. 127-128.) How does the dominant goal meet the three principles presented by Patterson to best achieve the ideal of self-realization? (p. 129.)

11. It has been stated that complete self-realization may never be achieved in one's lifetime. Teachers of physical education and coaches of sport often set high objectives or goals for themselves or for their students to achieve. Of what significance or value are goals that cannot be completely achieved? (pp. 127-128.)

12. Does obedience to the rules of the sport frequently involve self-denial, hardship, self-sacrifice, and the relinquishing of one's personal desires? What benefits are to be derived to oneself through making sacrifices for the benefit of the team? Why should one relinquish personal desires in order that others may benefit? (pp. 128-129.)

13. If self-sacrifice for one's teammates and/or the team means an irreparable loss to the individual, can you support it as a duty which one can perform? Consider, as an example, receiving a physical injury in the act of protecting a teammate or, in scoring the winning goal, an injury which terminates the sophomore's sport career. How would this question be an-

swered by the theorist who supports (1) devotion to duty, (2) the competitive struggle for power, (3) human development and self-realization, (4) the pursuit of happiness, and (5) authoritarianism?

14. Applying the five selected theories presented in this chapter, how would you identify and descriptively indicate the athletic coach who intensively drives the athletes to an extreme degree of physical, mental, and emotional exertion and to the disregard of their personal welfare with only the goal of winning in mind? Is it possible to bring into harmony any of the features of the theories so as to support the actions of the coach or to condemn the actions of the coach?

15. When one makes personal sacrifices in order that the team may benefit, he or she also takes steps toward the realization of a larger and more inclusive self. That is, one becomes more conscious of the relationship between self-sacrifice and achievement of a cause. When the team triumphs through winning, the individual also triumphs because of being associated with the particular cause. But what if the team loses? Or what if the team consistently wins game after game? Does the individual athlete gain anything after his or her own personal consciousness of self if this relationship subsides? (pp. 126-128.)

16. The final high school football game of the season was always held between cross-town, traditional rivals amidst highly emotional circumstances. In the early part of the second half of the game, the all-state fullback was shaken up on a hard tackle and removed from the game. There is an athletic trainer present but no physician. The player's symptoms evidence a possible head concussion. The trainer advises the player not to be re-entered. Ten seconds remain in the game and the score 6 to 0 in favor of the visiting team. The ball is on the four-yard line of the visiting team and in possession of the home team. The coach turns to the injured fullback and asks if he feels well enough to enter the game and run the last play in an effort to score the needed touchdown. The player, emotionally involved and wanting so much to win the game, indicates he can do so. The coach then sends the fullback in for the final play.

Which of the ethical theories best describes the coach and the coach's motives in this instance?

17. Is deviation from the rules and policies agreed upon for sport necessary in order to win contests? If your answer is *no,* how do you account for the wide differences in the standings of teams in a conference at the end of a season, or in the national rankings? Shouldn't each team of a conference, all of whom have agreed to abide by the established rules which are made by and for all conference members and intended to equalize conditions of operation, finish in a tie with all others in the conference?

18. Consider the following ethical incidents. Discuss each incident in terms of a description of the persons involved (teacher, coach, player) relative to ethical theories presented in this chapter. How would you classify each of the teachers, coaches, or players in each incident?

A. A high school teacher of history who also coached an athletic team could provide preferential treatment to members of the team when in class and in responsibilities unrelated to athletics. Team members who were in the after-lunch section individually spent their time at the teacher-coach's desk in consultation and reviewed tactics, strategy, and technique of play, while the rest of the class were given a reading assignment. The student-players who were in the last period of the day were excused from class in order to report to the practice area and secure early warm-ups. All such student-players received high grades for history.

B. At a recent NCAA swimming championship meet, the swimmers of a major independent university — that is, one which doesn't maintain membership in a conference — were informed by their coach that if they did not score points in the final events that day their athletic scholarships would be terminated at the end of the semester and would not be renewed for the next year. All these swimmers were citizens of another country whom they had represented in the Olympic Games. The removal of the financial aid meant a forced return to their own country without completing their university education. Up to this point in the championships, no member of this particular team had scored any points. However, the only ones threatened with the loss of aid were the international students. The reply given in justification of such a decision was (1) expectations from this group were greater than from others on the team, and (2) the action was legal since the university did not belong to a conference and was free of restricting rules.

C. Winning a contest can become so important as to overweigh in importance possible deleterious effects on an individual participant. In such instances, individual persons can become a means to an end, the end being winning.

For example, the wrestling team approaches the end of the season meeting their most difficult opponent in the conference. The outcome of the match determines the conference team champion. The home team's outstanding heavyweight wrestler is injured with a badly swollen and infected knee. Under ordinary conditions the wrestler would not be entered in the competition. The coach, however, suits-up both the wrestler and the number two, or less efficient, heavyweight. At the end of the 191-pound match, the team scores are tied. It is obvious that the number two heavyweight can not win the match. The coach, after consulting with the injured wrestler, enters him in the final match on the hope or expectation that things will work out to the home team's advantage.

D. The physical education teacher, who also coaches basketball, uses the instructional period in physical education as a means of securing extra time for basketball team practice. While the team members in the class practice under the coach's direction, the remaining members of the class are required to sit in the bleachers or are sent to the study hall.

E. The basketball coach of the visiting team becomes exasperated over what is termed very poor officiating during a particular game. As a protest against the officials' decisions, the visiting team coach removes the first starting team and replaces them with substitutes for the remainder of the game. Then, with the score at 91 to 34 in favor of the home team and with forty-five seconds remaining in the game, the coach calls time out in order to talk with the playing guard. When the game resumes, the guard, on instructions received from the visiting coach, runs to the home team basket and intentionally sinks five consecutive baskets for the opponents. The score now is raised above the century mark (101 to 34) for the opponents. The effect on the players of the losing team is depressing.

F. The Associated Press reported out of Minneapolis that for the first time in the United States a professional athlete was tried on a criminal charge for an incident that occurred during a sports contest. Boston Bruins' Al Jones was indicted and tried for allegedly hitting North Stars' hockey player Jim Green with his hockey stick on January 4. The assault resulted in a serious injury. The trial ended on July 18 in a hung jury. Jurors said the final vote had been 9 to 3 in favor of conviction on a lesser charge of simple assault. Jones was suspended for ten games without pay following the fight. The prosecutor declared that Jones "behaved in a dangerous manner towards another person, but he is not a danger to society."

Chapter 4

THE APPLICATION OF ETHICAL THEORIES TO SELECTED ANOMIES* IN PHYSICAL EDUCATION AND SPORT

I. WINNING IS THE ONLY THING

THE doctrine *winning is the only thing* evolved out of the sport environment in a highly competitive atmosphere that dominated a culture and in a time when it experienced an initial receptivity by sport adherents. Its ethical and moral implications were somewhat subdued in view of the acknowledged success achieved by the primary sources which enunciated the statement. That is, within the culture generally and in sport particularly, there has been widespread acceptance of the pragmatic experience that success is determined by status achieved at the top.

The win-loss record provides the primary basis for a judgment related to successful achievement. It provides recognition to the elements of personal character which undergirds the doctrine such as self-denial and sacrifice of self to the attainment of a single-minded goal or motive. The achievement record subscribes to the development of selfhood through complete subjection of self to an ultimate goal or consequence. If we acknowledge the inseparability between motives, means, and consequences in ethical or moral acts of a practical nature and attempt to determine what is right by viewing the doctrine in this relationship, we may better form a judgment on the acceptability or rejection of the doctrine.

Reference to the substance of any single ethical theory is inadequate in seeking a rationale to support or reject the doctrine. However, there are important elements of substance

---

Anomies — A state of society in which normative standards of conduct and belief have weakened or disappeared.

138

within several theories which will help to contribute to thinking about the statement and assist in forming a decision or judgment about it. A consideration of extracts from the theories may also help one to secure a broader perspective of the doctrine and cause questions to be raised concerning its applicability to the entire range of human action and life.

We shall, therefore, look at the elements of authoritarianism, naturalism (struggle for power), and self-realization and the development of self. We shall recognize that the primary challenge to the doctrine of *winning is the only thing* will issue from the philosophical and ethical views of the individual and self-realization theory. But we shall not omit whatever supporting components there might be within other existing ethical theories in order to secure as comprehensive a view of the doctrine as can be provided in this brief treatment.

The ethical analysis of the doctrine will be made by examining its major components, that is, *winning* as a human endeavor and winning as the *only* thing.

Self-Realization as the Base for Judgment

The essence of the ethics of self-realization is the fulfillment or realization of the capacities and potentialities which are present in the human nature of each person. This standard for the development of persons as human beings is represented in the goals of educational institutions and is found in the code of ethics of educational organizations. It is also found in the principles which issue from the foundations of a democratic society that views above all else the dignity and humanness of the individual person as the end for which all else exists. Self-realization maintains the fundamental postulate of the worth of persons and places emphasis on the social as well as the personal implications of the total personality. It recognizes the need for the harmonious development of all components of the human personality and considers all actions which contribute to this purpose to be morally good.

Physical education and sport have long subscribed to the tenets of this theory. The person has been and is viewed as an organismic and harmonious whole while acknowledging the individuality and uniqueness of each person. The components of self that comprise the person's nature function in a completely integrated manner so as to make up one's total personality and is influenced by an ultimate source of value in terms of goodness and right.

How, then, does the pursuit of winning and the experience of winning contribute to assisting one to realize one's capacities and potentialities? The case to be presented here is one which takes an affirmative view concerning the pursuit of an ideal or goal, including that of winning. The case of whether or not winning is the only thing is yet to be considered.

The Pursuit of Winning

The self-realization theory recognizes that, in the process of pursuit, loyalty to an ideal integrates the components of self into a harmonious whole. The establishment of a central task or goal, in preference to other goals, and the subordination of lesser though related and contributory goals assists one to mobilize and synthesize all efforts and energies toward achieving that goal. The intense devotion of self to the achievement of winning in sport represents an excellent example of this process. The development of loyalty to a supreme cause and the subjection of oneself in whatever way is needed to realize that cause often requires high degrees of self-denial and sacrifice of self in the devotion to all ancillary tasks which contribute to the end of winning.

The emphasis here is upon the process of striving to achieve the established goal of winning rather than the ultimate capture of the goal itself.

The type of devotion to a cause which takes a person out of the routine of life's daily round of activities that have a mere selfish and transitory significance may be identified by the sportsman in pursuit of the goal of winning. If one enlists his or her energies toward a goal which is considered good in terms of the contextual environment in which the goal exists, that is, written rules of the contest which direct human behavior of socially acceptable ways, one is able to give life direction and purpose. It is recognized, of course, that possibilities in the pursuit of the goal of winning may also be morally bad as well as in ways that are of ethical value.

Royce[32] indicated that genuine loyalty to a cause of a moral kind is one whose causes contribute to the over-all harmonious life of the great community of mankind as a whole. It can, therefore, be universalized as Kant would have it in the categorical imperative by translating the formula from a logical criterion of consistency into a maxim of goodness or rightness of action in terms of ultimate social worth.

Here again we are referring to winning not as the ultimate goal but to the *process* of pursuing the goal and to the degree of devotion to this particular cause.

Royce[24] provided a deep insight into the pursuance of a cause with purpose as one which unifies others in its service.

> Such is the cause. That the individual loves it is, in any case, due to the chances of his temperament and his development. That it can be conceived and served is a matter of social experience; that it is more worthy to be served than are any passing whims, individual or social, is the insight which the individual gets whenever he surveys his life in its wider unities. That to serve it requires creative effort; that it cannot be served except by positive deeds is the result of all one's knowledge of it. That in such service one finds self-expression even in and through self-surrender, and is more of a self even because one gives one's self, is the daily experience of all who have found such a cause. That such service enables one to face fortune with a new courage, because, whatever happens to the servant to the cause, he is seeking not his own fortune, but that of the cause, and has therefore discounted his own personal defeats. (Pp. 283-284)

Does the End Justify the Means?

There is often a hesitancy to answer the question, Does the end justify the means? because it is thought that until all circumstances in the total situation are considered, a decision should be deferred. This hesitancy implies that there may be instances where the end does justify the means that are employed to achieve the ultimate goal. Titus and Keeton[39] have indicated that it is a question that cannot be answered categorically yes or no, but that each case must be judged on its merits. These authors present a principle to govern decisions in cases where the comparative merit of means and ends is to be judged: "Use that combination of end and means that is the most beneficial possible to those affected directly or indirectly" (p. 101). The combination of a high motive, through the application of a good means, to results that are beneficial represents the basic factors in judging whether or not conduct is right. The absence of any of these factors in the combination will lead to moral censure.

An example of judging each case on the basis of its own merits may be illustrated. The subjection of participants in sport to excessive and rigorous training schedules and long periods of practice in preparation for a contest may not in themselves represent an evil means employed in an attempt to win. However, in the case of re-entering an athlete into a contact sport such as football after having received a brain concussion in the same contest would be disapproved as a means of attempting to win. In this latter case, where a possible fatal or near fatal injury can occur, the use of a human being in an effort to win represents the use of a means which outweighs any value to be achieved from winning as the end result. If one is to consider the *person* as the end for which sport exists rather than sport as the end for which the person exists, then exclusive and total support must be accorded the philosophy that games and contests within an educational climate (that is sponsored by schools and colleges) exists for the purpose of educating the participant.

The person-as-the-end rather than the person-as-the-means philosophy is consistent with the principles of self-realization which acknowledge the person as the end toward which all facets of life contribute. This belief is also consistent with the foundational principles of a democratic society in which the person is recognized as the end. The belief is particularly appropriate in the realm of sport and physical education which reside within and are approved and sponsored by educational institutions. Any force or factor which operates in the educational environment which attempts to use the person to achieve other ends is directly contrary to the concept that educational programs should serve the person, rather than the reverse. In a communistic or totalitarian society, the person serves as a *means* to meet the needs of the state, the state representing the end. In a democratic society, the state serves as a means to serve the person, the person being the end.

The prevalence of a concept such as that which is expressed in the statement "winning is the only thing" undermines the concept of the supremacy and dignity of the individual personality and is inconsistent with the concepts that are advanced in the self-realization theory.

Winning as the Only Thing Within the Context of Authoritarianism

The environment of authoritarianism is one in which the doctrine of *winning is the only thing* flourishes. Here is witnessed a sharp contrast between the dominant motives of survival wherein strict rules of conduct are decreed by those in power versus happiness and self-realization wherein the rules of conduct represent a consensus among equals. A united effort to win as the *only* goal requires uncritical conformity. Ethical reasoning or questions of right or wrong, if any may be raised, terminate with an authority whose might makes decisions right. Grievance rights and procedures are nonexistent.

It is to be noted that authoritarianism as an accepted force in the scheme to promote winning as the *only* thing succeeds in an environment where the objective of winning, under the *only* condition, is unanimously accepted by the group and is recognized as of paramount importance. Social solidarity which develops in the process of working toward the goal and under this special condition results in a centralized structure form and a rigid pattern of binding rules of conduct. Discipline and loyalty to the cause are indoctrinated. The ethical and moral rules are fixed by the rigid rules of the authoritarian source. The ideals of self-realization are condemned or abandoned because they distract from the solidarity theme.

Questions that may be raised at this point are, What of the individual? What of the potentialities for realizing one's self? Are there, in such a setting, possibilities available to the individual to make decisions or choices related to his or her expression based on free will? The answers are, of course, negative ones because the condition of *only* which exists in the doctrine represents a complete exclusiveness of any or all extraneous factors in the process. The standard of goodness which is concerned with the harmonious development of the human personality and the recognition of individuality and uniqueness are sublimated to the supreme goal of winning in which *all* factors, including individual persons, must serve as a means. All factors which exist in self or in human nature — body, mind, desires for human and material wants, enrichment knowledges and understandings, and ideals — must be directed toward the single-minded goal.

Finally, when winning becomes the only thing, there follows a reversal in the order of importance of values, which under different conditions would permit one to approximate the ideals of self-realization. Thus, the extrinsic values of power, prestige, money, and status replace the intrinsic values expressed in spiritual good; the transient values which rise from the senses or are sensual (gratification, self-satisfaction) replace values of a permanent nature related to the ideals or spirit of a person; and values that are ends in themselves and nonproductive of other values replace those which enrich the lives of others in a consequential and continuous manner.

Winning as the Only Thing Within the Context of Naturalism (Struggle for Power)

Winning as the *only* thing embraces that facet of naturalistic philosophy which recognizes self-interest as the dominant motive in each person. It stems out of the context of a struggle for power, recognition, survival, or security. Each group or person seeks to fulfill his or her own nature and acts in competition with everyone else. Since individual interests clash with one another, they all cannot reach their goals. Some are going to lose out, and their welfare will be sacrificed to others in order that others may gain their own ends. Not everyone can win. Excluding ties, only 50 percent can win. The expectations are that those who are stronger than their competitors will achieve the results that accrue from winning, while the losers, the weaker ones, will have to get along as best they can. *Might makes right* is this particular doctrine. Cooperative relationships are undertaken only to preserve the existence of the primary motive, which is winning, of the individual or group.

The goal of winning can often become of paramount importance to the exclusion of all other values. A means of achieving the goal among those who comprise a conference or who seek an objective which is available only to the winner (such as national recognition, a post-season tournament, a title bid, or a conference title) may be indicated by the following principle:

> The unit which surpasses the limits of the established and approved practices of the group invariably wins out.*

An apt illustration of the principle in actual operation has been recorded by a former football coach of a prominent college team who stated, "Until three years ago we obeyed every rule, and where did it get us? We finished last in the conference. Since that time there isn't a rule we haven't broken. And where are we now? This year we're playing in the Orange Bowl."

That such unethical practices are applied in other spheres of human endeavor is indicated by a well-known professor of international politics.[16] He wrote cogently of the relationship between power, principle, and world order by expressing, "Whenever peace conceived as the avoidance of war has been the primary objective of a group of powers, the international system has been at the mercy of the most ruthless member of the international community. Whenever the international order

---

Unit = an individual, team, school, corporation, state, nation, etc.; *Established and approved practices* = the rules collectively agreed upon by the group to govern their procedures and behavior in striving toward common goals (winning, profits, peace, etc.); *Group* = a collection of units, all of whom come together for common purposes.

has acknowledged that certain principles could not be compromised even for the sake of peace, stability based on an equilibrium of forces was at least conceivable" (p. 1).

The inclusion of the word *only* in the doctrine that *winning is the only thing* supports that statement, "the end justifies the means." That is, whatever practical results are to be achieved, any means are justified in achieving them. To achieve the end of winning involves no obligation to be honest, truthful, and obedient to the rules of the game or of the organization, be it conference, national association, intramural leagues, or class. If adherence to these qualities can produce winning performances, then apply them. If they do not produce desired results, then abandon them for whatever qualities will. If deceit, cruelty, and injustice are effective, it is proper to employ them.

Those who wish to exist in the environment of winning as the *only* thing must adapt to that environment or cease to survive. Since all compete for this *only* goal in the environment, only those who possess the greater strength or ingenuity to beat out their competitors will succeed. The process embraces Darwin's theory of the struggle for existence and survival of the fittest.

Weiss[41] presents a contrast between the objectives and the means of achieving them that exist in war and in a game. While the objective of a game is the production of results acceptable to both sides, the objective of a war is a defeat of the enemy. The chief difference between them is the subjugation of participants by injury or destruction and the breaking of their economic, social, and political power by war, while victory in athletics is the exhibition of excellence even in those defeated. Weiss states,

> Everything is allowed in a war if victory thereby results; a
> victor in a game is to be denied victory if there has been a
> failure to abide by some essential rule. (p. 180)

There is sometimes such an occurrence that two or more competitors as individuals or teams may be equalized with no variations among them. They compete, therefore, to a tie. The naturalists recognize the existence of an on-going struggle, not for the immediate present, but for the long-term adaptation to the environment and to the long-term struggle for survival and achievement in that environment. In other words, the struggle does not cease with the immediate contest but continues into the future with continued efforts to employ added means to win.

It is disconsolate to those who embrace a humanitarian philosophy and who support conventional morality and democracy in the approach to working with other humans to observe the doctrine of *winning is the only thing*. This would seem to be especially so when one views as applicable under the *only* provision the Nietzsche struggle for power theory. The *only* good to strive for in the higher stages of evolution is winning. The will to power and success through winning is to use persons or any other means to acquire more of winning. One may resort to deceit, cruelty, and violence to achieve it. Exploitation and deception will be employed if such practices seem appropriate.

It is of interest to note that out of the application of the doctrine of Nietzsche there arise classes of people or groups, out of which evolve a sort of master and slave morality. This concept recognizes that persons will belong to different ranks and will not be equal. Each rank will have a different set of rules or moral principles for each of the separate classes, and the rules will not be binding on all. This is not a particularly unknown concept when applied to sport. The establishment of divisions of sport teams for the purpose of equalization of competition based upon the basic purposes or motives of financial income and expenses, power, notoriety, and prestige is an actuality.

The democratic ideal of holding the individual person as of infinite worth and as the end for which all else exists was anathema to Nietzsche. His morality would recognize a leadership of supermen and superwomen with their own values, while the weaker ones would group together for self-protection and for their own interests against the stronger and more powerful.

The application and acceptance of the naturalist doctrines to sport which exist in educational institutions, such as secondary schools, colleges, and universities, is highly questionable and difficult to define. Such institutions uphold as their supreme goal the culturing of those factors which contribute to the development of the human person and the perfection of his and her functions. They totally support the humanistic concept that human beings as persons exist as *ends* in themselves and never as a *means* only.

II. EVERYONE ELSE IS DOING IT

The basic reasons which support the statement that "everyone else is doing it" are (1) to provide justification for actions which are contrary to established rules or imperatives, (2) that because others may be doing it, it is permissable for me to do it and therefore achieve an equality of conditions, or (3) to intentionally seek an advantage over others irrespective of the practices of others.

The primary thrust for treating this particular ethical incident will be extracted from the ethical theories of Kant and the concept of duty.

The clue to the discovery of Kant's *Moral Law* is provided by testing the rule (maxim) by universalizing it. The law is expressed as "I ought never to act except in such a way that I can also will that my rule (maxim) should become a universal law." The important point is that one should act in accordance with rules, principles, or imperatives that one recognizes as valid for everyone else. People claim no right for themselves that they don't admit as being right for others also. The entire ethics of the situation stands on conformity to rules whose validity and rightness is established through (1) their applicability to all rational beings and (2) one's ability to apply the rules and live with them and not contradict oneself by being inconsistent (i.e., to recognize the rules but then apply practices which are contrary to the rules and their educational intent).

The concept of duty applied to ethical behavior is not one conceived with how people *do* behave, but with how they *ought* to behave. Ought implies duty, and if persons were not conscious to duty there would be no discretionary actions related to value decisions. Without concern for *what should be* (ought) in a moral sense, there would be no morality.

The Intent and Nature of Rules

Rules which are intended to provide equity for all participants and teams in sport are unconditional. In this sense they constitute imperatives and are thus meant to be applied universally; they are the products of reason when applied to everyone, and they are rational and objective. It is only through their universality or through their applicability to everyone that their true validity can be tested. The true test of morality of the imperatives in sport that are concerned with such matters as the starting dates for team practice, recruiting and subsidizing of student-athletes, and adherence to academic and scholarship standards, among others, lies in the degree of intent to which they provide for fairness in treatment and the equalization of the practices of everyone so as not to permit some to secure an unfair advantage over others. The test of ethics becomes an extremely severe one in an environment of intense competition for producing winning performances. The test of morality, then, becomes not a test of the ethical imperative but of the individual persons who are expected to comply with the imperative.

There is no denial of the acceptability of the moral imperatives associated with the administration of sport. Those who would challenge the validity of the imperatives which pertain to their applicability to all rational beings would find difficulty in defending their views on the same criteria of rationality and universality. This is not to say that persons cannot formulate their own subjective rules or principles for themselves relative to their own goals, desires, or thoughts as long as these rules or principles are not binding on others. But these subjective rules are not imperatives that meet the criteria established in Kant's theory related to the categorical imperative. Kant recognized no *ifs* or *ors,* as in statements of counsels of prudence, but instead maintained that categorical imperatives are duty binding.

One can better understand the difficulties that are encountered in attempting to interpret rules and related behavior when one views only isolated actions. Is it proper to start basketball practice prior to October 15 when the rules explicitly state that the practice period starts on October 15? What difference do two or three weeks make in starting earlier, especially when others are doing the same thing? There are always ways of circumventing the spirit of the rules. For example, the basketball team can, prior to the stated starting practice date, practice *informally* under the direction of a graduate assistant while the coach sits in the stands exerting influence in a sort of remote control manner. The same conditions and questions may be presented in viewing similar practices related to other sports which maintain rules related to practice dates.

The Test for Rules

The deviation from rules of conduct in isolated situations may seem to be a relatively small matter and is passed off with the thought that everyone else is doing it. When one magnifies the consequences of such thoughts and actions by universalizing them and comparing the consequences in relation to the original intention of the imperatives, one can then easily discern the ramifications of the results. It seems incongruous to condone practices which are inconsistent with the educational and ethical intentions of imperatives which are designed to provide conditions of equality and equity for *all* individuals and *all* programs in order to maintain well-structured programs with an integrity of purpose.

If imperatives possess internal inconsistencies when universally applied, then they are irrational and therefore not valid. They should then be subject to change. But the test of rationality and consistency must be applied to the original purpose for which the imperatives were designed. It is not enough to say that because *everyone else is doing it* the practice must be O.K., and therefore the imperative should be changed to permit everyone to adopt a consistent practice. The concept of rationality and consistency implies the importance of possessing knowledge and understanding of the true educational and ethical intentions of imperatives and their relationship to the context of practices in physical education and sport. What, for example, is the intention of rules which require students to adhere to standards related to the need to academically progress quantitatively and qualitatively toward degree attainment, or to maintain stated levels of academic performance for eligibility to participate in extracurricular activities, including sports? Such rules represent a means of providing assurance that the primary function and purpose of educational institutions will be met. This is particularly so in relation to the role of the institution in contributing to the continuing intellectual development of the students and in preparing a well-informed, intelligent, active, and contributing citizen for this nation.

Thus internal consistency and rationality in the relationships between the educational intent of imperatives and existing practices provides the best criteria for judging the acceptability of the statement, "everyone else is doing it." Failure to comply with the imperatives which are based upon this criteria leads to an undermining of the educational nature of physical education and sport and to the deterioration of the relationship between individuals and institutions which constitute important elements in the functioning of our democratic society.

Kant goes somewhat farther than what has been indicated by stating that it is not enough to outwardly conform to the imperatives. There is no ethical or moral worth unless one's impulses and actions are guided and supported by a rational will. In other words, one doesn't comply with the rules simply because a person must comply or else suffer from imposed sanctions. Rather, one should comply with the imperatives because they are recognized as the directives for right and proper actions, that is, the right thing to do. They should clearly support the understood relationship between the intent of the imperatives and the proper practices. Thus, a person's actions are based upon a voluntary, rational will to do the proper thing because one truly feels it is proper.

The Incompatibility of Rules and Practices

How does one reconcile the seeming incompatibility between

established rules, codes, and laws with a persisting conduct which functions under the justification that the rules and codes are unrealistic, that *everyone else is doing it,* and that it is a natural impulse to seek advantage of others in a highly competitive environment? Within such an environment, the causes of conduct which are incompatible to well-intended rules become obvious.

However, when emphasis is placed on the causes of such conduct, it provides excuses for transgressions. Such transgressions, whose intent can never be hidden from the participants, erode the concept of personal and professional responsibility of teachers and coaches and directly affect the quality of future leadership. For example, one should not expect individual performers in physical education and sport who themselves will one day be placed into teaching and coaching positions to apply practices different from what they were subjected to during their own periods of performance. Such conduct patterns are especially relevant in circumstances which function under the justification that actions are considered to be right because *everyone else is doing it.*

There may be only a short distance from functioning under such leadership to becoming a leader oneself. The rules and codes are adopted because of the perceived need to place restraints on human frailties, not to accommodate them.

The practices which endure under the concept of *everyone else is doing it* point up the distinct incompatibility between the purposes of sport, when administered under a philosophy which places winning at such a high premium, and the primary purposes of educational institutions and their programs, which strive for equality of conditions under which univerally recognized educational principles and practices are applied. A seemingly wise policy to be applied in both areas of sport and education would be to try to mitigate the impact of differences in principles, policies, and practices related to the equality of conditions which cultivate the growth of jointly recognized educational objectives. This is not meant to underestimate the beneficial effects of maintaining and supporting the goal of winning; each institution strives for excellence and, in the process, urges commensurate performances from all of its components.

This incompatibility does point up a continued need to not only provide for consistency and harmony between all components of the educational process, but to protect and culture the indispensable basis upon which a free and organized society rests, namely, the elements of trust and respect both for each other and for the processes of education.

Perhaps nowhere in contemporary sport is there a more vivid

Figure 8. One of the damaging effects of violence in sport has been that on young aspiring athletes who look to their heroes for guidance and example. (Photo courtesy of United Press International, Inc.)

example of the incompatibility between established rules and codes and personal conduct than that exhibited in the scenes of violent behavior of performers and fans. The major ignition to the conflagration is lack of sportsmanship and ethical behavior among athletes, coaches, and spectators. Although violence in hockey has attracted the greatest attention, similar incidents in other sports have also caused widespread concern, suggesting both the inadequacy of disciplining mechanisms of organizations which conduct sports and the need for some form of deterence. One of the damaging effects has been that on young aspiring athletes who look to their heroes for guidance and example.

DISCUSSION TOPICS

1. What changes would need to occur in our society in order to *lessen* the degree of acceptance of the pragmatic experience that success is determined by status achieved at the top?

2. On what basis can you reconcile the win-loss record in sport as a judgment related to successful achievement with other factors that might transcend the win-loss syndrome? What might some of these other factors be?

3. How much public acceptance is there of the losing coach's claims to character development as a factor in reconciling the losing season?

4. In which of the ethical theories presented in Chapter 3 do you find the greatest support for the doctrine of *winning is the only thing?* In which ethical theory do you find the least support? Present your primary points in support and lack of support for your selection.

5. How does the devotion of self in the pursuit of winning contribute toward assisting one to realize one's capacities and potentialities as conceived in the self-realization theory? (p. 140.)

6. There are those who, after having achieved their ultimate goal, claim that the entire process of striving with its high degree of self-denial, self-sacrifice, and hardship, together with supreme loyalty to the cause, is more rewarding than the ulti-

mate capture of the goal itself. How would you explain this expression in terms of the theory of self-realization? (p. 140.)

7. Contrast the two methods used to develop world class performers in sport: that used by the United States representing a democratic culture and that of the Soviet Union and East Germany which represent a communistic culture. Which of the two extremely different philosophies is most likely to prove the most effective in the production of winning performances in sport? Fully support your contention (p. 143.)

8. Contrast the two statements "winning is the *only* thing" and "winning is the *most important* thing." Wherein lie the differences in these two concepts? Describe circumstances where you could justify the latter of the two concepts. As an educator (teacher and coach), what important facts must you maintain in your thinking in an environment where either one or both of these concepts prevail? (pp. 146-147.)

9. Look carefully at the principle on p. 145 relative to one means of achieving the goal of winning. Note the illustration which follows the statement of the principle. You are asked to universalize this principle, that is, apply it to all of life and all of the interrelations between people. What would you expect the results to be?

10. What is the intent of high school associations in establishing rules pertaining to the length and dates of practice and playing seasons and the number of contests? If there is rather widespread misapplication of these rules because of the reasoning "everyone else is doing it," would such practices justify a change in the rules? What are the reasons for your replies?

11. What measures would seem necessary to currently curtail and prevent future occurrences of violence in sport? What effects are the demonstrations of violent behavior in sport expressed by performers and spectators likely to have on young aspiring athletes who look to their heroes for guidance and example? (p. 154.)

Chapter 5

THE ETHICAL INCIDENT IN
PHYSICAL EDUCATION AND SPORT

$\mathbf{T}$HE ethical incident approach in physical education and sport makes it possible for one to become highly involved in the ethical study experience. An incident serves as a central core around which revolve all the elements described in the *Method of Ethical Judgment and Principle Construction* presented in Chapter 2. In a sense, the incident approach serves as a simple yet well-structured manner of synchronizing a validated method for ethical discussions. The incident serves as the focus of attention for questions or discussions which permit individuals to examine their own personal values and feelings and to develop their own perspectives.

The sample incident presented in this chapter brings the teacher-coach of the potential state championship basketball team to a point of decision making that will affect his or her future professional and personal life. The decision may as well have a profound effect upon those in the school and community. There are plentiful samplings of similar incidents at the end of each chapter in the text that may be placed into a position for further description and analysis. Students may, however, develop their own incidents out of personal experiences or from a wide variety of media.

The ethical incident, then, constitutes the major resource out of which one arrives at ethical judgments. These judgments subsequently form a basis for establishing universal ethical principles. The ethical incident describes a problem-solving situation involving two or more ethical issues from which one must make a decision as to choice of decision or action. An incident most often involves a conflict between possible alternative ways of choosing between what may be considered right or wrong. The consequences of the judgment will have a direct effect upon persons involved in or by the incident. The incident places the central figure who must make the judgment into the situation of intellectually experiencing the eight coordinated and sequential steps that are presented in Figure 3 (The Method of Ethical Judgment, p. 45).

OPERATIONAL CRITERIA FOR AN ETHICAL INCIDENT

The objective operational criteria for an ethical incident are as follows:

1. It presents a realistic conflict for the decision maker.
2. It must include a number of ethical issues or conflicts.
3. Its alternatives should be clearly susceptible to being judged by criteria for rightness.
4. It should yield a series of consequences which directly relate to the alternatives of action or decision.
5. It should create cognitive conflict among the deliberators of the incident so as to reflect a variety of value judgments related to alternatives, rightness, and consequences.
6. It should, upon consideration by a number of deliberators (such as students in a class), generate differences in judgment or opinion regarding the choice made by the decision maker.

An ethical incident should not be considered in a casual manner. It needs to be very carefully structured and, preferably, presented in written form. All of the pertinent circumstances need to be considered with due regard for the inclusion of all of the facts.

ELEMENTS OF AN ETHICAL INCIDENT

Every ethical incident will contain at least four major elements.

1. The Conceptual Phase

First, there will be the conceptualizing of all cognitive data. This process might be considered as a *focus of ethicalization* and is represented in Step Two of *The Method of Ethical Judg-*

THE STRUCTURAL RELATIONSHIP BETWEEN
THE COMPONENTS OF
THE ETHICAL REASONING PROCESS

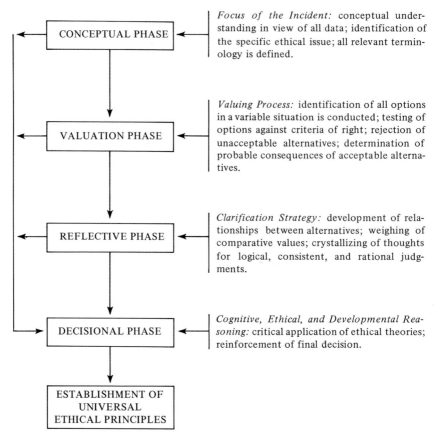

Figure 9.

ment. It requires that a comprehensive understanding (that is, conceptualization) of the situation, problem, or dilemma which is to be examined takes place. The exact nature of the incident and the specific ethical issue involved in it are to be identified. All relevant data are to be collected which may not have been available at the time the incident was first presented. It is important for the decision maker and everyone else who is involved in the ethical judgment experience to demonstrate their understanding of the incident in view of all available data. It is important that everyone who will share in the ethical incident experience be aware of the conflict between the ethical positions. Until all are aware of the conflict, the incident can only be considered as described. This phase also includes the conceptual understanding of the relevant terminology to be used, such as *right, truth, honesty, justice,* etc. There needs to be evidence of the first phase of the process. In this way, there will be some assurance that all adequately understand and can conceptualize the focus of the study around which ethical reasoning may take place toward making an ethical judgment.

The focus of the incident might take a number of forms. For example, it might be *philosophical* (winning is the only thing); involve *educational objectives* (neglect of teaching in favor of other interests or substitutes of other school activities for physical education); a *legal* issue (abuse of eligibility rules or actions involving the circumvention of the spirit of the rules of play but not the letter of the rules); a *social* or *problem-solving* situation (conflicts between the personal freedoms of the athlete versus the disciplinary nature of training); a *personal* dilemma (the use of drugs to enhance performance, or prejudices of discriminating against religion, color, or national origin, or favoritism and privileges granted for personal aggrandizement); a *misuse of scientific information* (the advertising or selling of gimmicks and gadgets for modification of the human body related to fitness, weight reduction, or body image purposes); or *constitutional rights* or *human rights* situations (the provision of a disproportionate share of resources for boys' and men's programs as against girls' and women's programs).

2. The Valuation Phase

The second major element is the Valuation Phase. This phase of the ethical incident projects the deliberation of the situation into the first of a series of three steps (see Fig. 3).

These three steps involve (1) the establishment of tentative hypotheses in terms of what *ought* to be the alternative decisions or actions in the situation, (2) the testing of these alternatives against the criteria or rightness with a subsequent rejection of those which do not adequately meet the criteria, and (3) the determination of the probable consequences of the acceptable alternatives.

The Valuation Phase of the ethical incident experience is similar in nature to the Valuing Process projected by Raths[30] and his associates wherein one may express preferences for or against certain ideas, behaviors, decisions, and alternatives. Options are identified in variable situations, the criteria by which value choices (in terms of rightness) are made are then constructed and applied, and the consequences which may be or should be considered are indicated before entering any decisional stage. It is during this stage that one has freedom of expression concerning personal feelings and verbal behavior. It is, in a real sense, an expression of valuing skills, that is, expressing one's own values from the entire range of values which are open.

One asks, what possible courses of action would seem most reasonable? (Refer to Step 3, p. 48.) Which of these possible courses of action could be considered the best alternatives in terms of the greatest possible good or least possible harm concerning the consequences for other or for all people? (Refer to Step 4, p. 49.) Of those options which are considered most acceptable, which ones show consequences whose values have the most educational implications for the welfare of the individual and group involved? (Refer to Step 5, p. 51.)

3. The Reflective Phase

The third major element is the Reflective Phase. The data used during this phase of the ethical incident are taken from the results of the previous two phases, namely, the Conceptual Phase and the Valuation Phase. Here the deliberator evaluates the probable consequences of each acceptable alternative which survived the critical test of rightness and attempts to understand the relationships between the alternatives and their consequences. An understanding of these factors helps one to reflect upon and reconsider one's understandings, relationships, and preferences. (Refer to Step 6, p. 52.) The process in the words of Raths[30] is appropriately labelled a *values clarification strategy* (pp. 3-12).

When a person enters the comparative evaluation experience in the ethical realm, one engages in reflective thinking. An appropriate question to ask is, To what degree or in what rank order might I list the right or best things to do? Here one weighs all the factors in an attempt to find a reasonable standard or principle to assist in answering the question. Reflection helps to gain perspective, to see relationships between alternatives, and to weigh comparative values of each of the alternatives. It renders personal thinking more systematic and enlightened, provides some basis for a rational judgment, and helps to crystallize one's thoughts to a point where a ranking of values becomes logical and consistent.

4. The Decisional Stage

The fourth major element is the Decisional Stage. This stage requires the deliberator to make a final decision and to reinforce it. It represents the culmination of reflection on the alternatives that have been identified in Stage Three. (Refer to Step 7, p. 54.)

This phase corresponds with Kohlberg's[17] sixth stage (Level III) of his cognitive moral development theory, namely, the Universal Ethical Principle Orientation. The final decision and its corresponding reinforcement represents the highest level of cognitive, moral, and developmental reasoning. The summary judgment finds its rationale in the original definition of a principle that was proposed in an earlier chapter, i.e., the determination of truth or ethical right which may serve to guide decisions or actions which involve the education and/or welfare of persons toward all that is good. It is in this state that one responds to a self-determined obligation to ethical principles that apply to all humankind. One's final judgment is based on the consequences of the decision in terms of the welfare of everyone involved with due regard to the universality of its application to all living organisms. Here the ethical concepts and principles such as equality, justice, or the dignity of the individual are brought to bear upon the process. One appeals to logic, comprehensiveness, universality, and consistency. It is here also that one finds roots in substantive ethical theories such as those that were presented from selected ethical systems in Chapter 3. This is particularly so in reference to the reinforcement of the final decision or choice of alternative. One must answer the questions, On what grounds is my judgment correct? What evidence is there that my judgment is a substantive one? To what sources might I refer to further strengthen the judgment preference? What reasons can be given to further support the ethical judgment?

The search for support for ethical judgments is distinctly philosophical with a strong reliance on the development of relationships between ethical theories, the basic and applied sciences, theology, and religion relative to human justice, law, deductive logic for self-evident principles, and other sources of data. It is out of the experience of the Decisional Stage that abstract ethical principles are derived, freely developed, and chosen by the individual because of their intrinsic ethical validity.

THE ROLE OF INTERROGATION IN ETHICAL REASONING

Reference to the schematic illustration (Fig. 10) will display a series of questions which are grouped under each of the four phases of the model. The purposes of these questions are to help organize the data and thinking around the incident being studied, while at the same time making it possible for a group to engage in a spontaneous and flexible type of expression. Otherwise, the discussion would likely wander, be disconnected, and be dominated by caprice. The provision of questions grouped under each of the major phases of the model encourages everyone who is involved in the discussion to participate, to express ideas, to share values and feelings, and to

A SCHEMATIC ILLUSTRATION OF AN ETHICAL REASONING
EXPERIENCE (ETHICAL INCIDENT) CULMINATING IN THE
ESTABLISHMENT OF UNIVERSAL ETHICAL PRINCIPLES

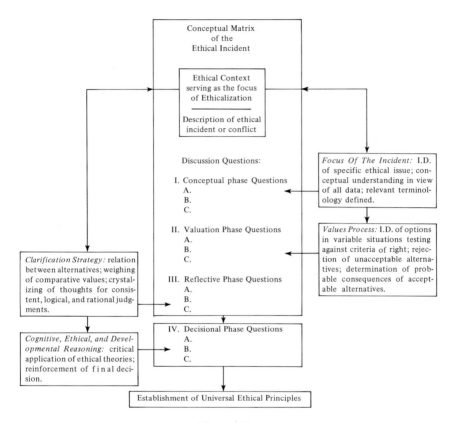

Figure 10.

refer to data in several of the phases with freedom of expression. The questions also encourage openness, yet an equalization of status in expressing one's personal values, beliefs, and preferences.

Specifically, the series of questions to be considered under each of the major phases serve the following purposes:

1. To share information and knowledge about the incident that is to be the object of valuation and decision making.
2. To permit a checking against statements presented by

others to assure that such statements are based on accurate information, rather than ill-founded personal opinion, biases, or inaccuracies.

3. To comprehend the incident and review the meaning of key words which may prove to be significant in bringing about a common understanding among all individuals involved in the incident experience.

4. To help generate, express, and elaborate on relationships between alternatives and a weighing of the comparative values of each.

5. To determine, objectify, and publicly state and affirm value ratings and preferences in a verbal way.

6. To better understand the choices and actions of others based upon their feelings and the degree of time and thought which they have given to their deliberations.

Although the questions are structured into the model, one does not need to feel that they have to be rigidly adhered to or followed in sequence. They are intended to be representative of the type of questions which should be asked during the process of reasoning of a typical ethical incident. There may be other questions to be considered; for example, reference to the type of questions which are presented in the example of the teacher-coach incident on pages 172-174 reveals that the questions are directly related to the four phases of the ethical reasoning experience.

The discussion questions, when placed into positions shown in Figure 10 and in the model on page 158, also serve the purpose of adding rationality to the method used to arrive at ethical principles. The questions are directly related to the objectives being sought. Without a logical sequence of interrogation, that is, without appraisal, one can only act routinely or blindly. The act of choosing always involves a test of inquiry and entails a means of validation whereby one's actions can be appraised and evaluated. This type of validation through interrogation lies at the heart of a method where appraisal and evaluation of choices are to be made.

A TENTATIVE CLASSIFICATION OF INCIDENTS

A review of a relatively large number of varied types of both ethical and unethical incidents which have occurred in physical education and sport has made it possible to present a tentative classification of representative situations. These are offered to assist one to develop and describe an incident in which an interest exists. Rather than having a ready-made incident provided, the student of the ethical study experience may develop his or her own.

The primary purpose of the classification is to establish a focus of the study around which ethical reasoning will take place before arriving at an ethical judgment. From the tentative classification provided, one may seek for or develop hundreds of incidents.

The tentative classification follows:

1. The disciplinary nature of training versus the freedoms of the athlete.
2. The absolute rules of the coach versus the need for flexibility in enforcement.
3. Adherence to the letter of the rules but not to the spirit or purpose of the rules.
4. Fan behavior toward players, officials, coaches, state high school association, and other educational personnel.
5. Player behavior toward fans, officials, and coaches, including means to enhance winning. Helpfulness to other players or teammates.
6. Officials' behavior toward fans, coaches, and players.
7. Coaches' decisions and actions toward players, officials, fans, and other coaches. Techniques to enhance winning.
8. Cheerleader behavior toward opponents and others.
9. Discrimination in terms of sex, color, national origin, religion, personal characteristics, class status, grade status.
10. Neglect of teaching in favor of other interests (ball tosser).
11. Substitution of other school activities for physical educa-

Figure 11. A single hair attached from the scalp determines the sex of the sports performer. A technique approved by the International Olympic Committee to settle ethical disputes related to illegal entries in international competition, it is an appropriate context to serve as a focus for moral reasoning.

tion instruction.

12. Favoritism or privileges granted to selected athletes by the coach for personal reasons or for self-benefits.
13. Violation of constitutional rights or human rights based upon deprivation of opportunities.
14. Imposition of rules by supervising teachers which are contrary to the student-teacher's sense of values.
15. Practices employed by college recruiting agents (coaches, alumni) in approaching high school athletes. The substance of inducements offered.
16. Use of other than natural training means to improve physical performance (drugs, blood boosting, steroids, etc.).
17. Special privileges and favorite treatment shown winning coaches without corresponding regard for effective teachers.
18. Practices related to academic eligibility provisions, such as grade changing, grade privileges, teacher favors, etc.
19. Officials', players', and teachers' strikes.
20. Obligations to a professional code of ethics versus the freedoms of personal life (on and off the job behavior).

A SUMMARY OF PROCEDURES IN ESTABLISHING AN ETHICAL INCIDENT

The following summary will assist one to fully treat an ethical incident while gaining a perspective of all relationships that are involved in the process.

1. Create a context for the incident (as the focus of ethicalization).
   a. Refer to the classification of incidents.
   b. Select a classification in which there exists a particular interest.
   c. Seek a variety of sources for a description of an incident which fits the classification selected. Sources may consist of personal or observed experiences or a variety of media. Media sources may be newspaper, periodicals, television shows, movies, cartoons, photos, etc.

2. Formulate questions for discussion purposes related to the described incident (these are indicated in the guidelines on the role of interrogation in ethical reasoning).
   a. The questions may follow the sequence suggested in the format and represented in the four phases of the reasoning experience (conceptual, valuation, reflective, and decisional).
3. Treat the discussion questions prior to the presentation before a group or in a class. Responses to the questions may be developed in written reports prior to open class or group discussion. Prior consideration permits one to devote some time to reflect on *what should be*.
4. Fully discuss the questions in class or before the group. These questions may be followed in the sequence in which they were developed. This process of discussion permits one to
   a. Express feelings and verbal behavior.
   b. Express preferences for or against ideas, decisions, or alternatives.
   c. Offer options to proposals.
   d. Gain perspective, see relationships, and weigh comparative values.
5. Reach a summary judgment or decision, if possible. The summary judgment or decision is *not* expected to be a group action.
   a. Each individual formulates his or her own decision in terms of how one views its application in accordance to the definition of a principle and with the guidelines offered in the Decisional Stage. One appeals to logic, comprehensiveness, universality, and consistency. Roots for decision making may be found in the substance of ethical theories.
6. Formulate a statement of principle.
   a. The statement or statements of principle rise out of a review of the total process, a process which represents the highest level of intellectual reasoning. The statement or statements should be designed to serve as guides for decisions or actions concerning the educa-

tion and/or welfare (right and good) of persons. They should be universal in application and freely chosen by the individual because of their intrinsic moral validity.

The following ethical incident is presented as an example of the application of the ethical reasoning experience illustrated in the Model in Figure 10.

THE ETHICAL INCIDENT*

THE TEACHER-COACH PERSONAL CONFLICT

Clarification of Concepts Prior to Considering the Specific Incident

The clarification of concepts and terms as they apply to this specific ethical incident will assist to prevent conflicts in the interpretation of important words and ideas. There are two groups of concepts, words, or terms. They are as follows:

1. Those which, while not ethical in nature, lie in juxtaposition to the incident and are indispensable in interpreting the ethical implications of the incident. Their relationship to the incident is so important that decisions which are to be finally made must lie within the context of this group of concepts or terms, which include the following:

   a. *Academic Standards.* Since the educational process occurs within an established structure (a school, for example) there exist goals and objectives toward which students are expected to work. It is also expected that teachers (and other personnel) will assist students to achieve these. These objectives might be referred to as academic standards because they indicate the levels of and for achievement related to the knowledges and understandings, and skills and abilities in the various subject matter areas.

   Identify these various levels of academic standards or

---

*The format for the presentation of the Ethical Incident is derived from Robert J. Stahl, *Values/Moral Education: A Synthesis Model*, pp. 39-41.

performance (in terms of grading if you wish) and indicate why such standards are maintained in educational institutions.

b. *Primary Goals of the School and of Education.* This concept views the responsibility of the school in terms of its ultimate responsibility to the individual student and to the community, state, and nation. It states its goals in broad terms. It recognizes the relationships of the goals to a moral commitment to humanity as well as to the development of the intellectual, social, cultural, physical, and vocational aspects and needs of the individual.

Identify some of these goals not alone in relation to the individual but to all of society.

2. Those which lie within the core of ethical conduct and behavior. Their definition and interpretation are essential in providing a proper direction for considering incidents which involve the education and/or welfare of persons. Consider, for example, such terms as they apply to this particular incident:

a. Honesty
b. Integrity
c. Obligation to others
d. Equal rights for all
e. Justice
f. Injustice
g. Compromise
h. Threat to security
i. Responsibility to one's family

Define and discuss the above terms so as to secure clarification prior to proceeding with the incident which follows.

The Context of the Ethical Incident

The basketball team of Robinson High School experienced its most successful season in the history of the school this year. The people of the rural community in which the school is located are extremely proud of the team and its accomplishments, particularly since it has qualified for the state tournament. The community of Robinson has never before received such state-wide notoriety and feels that the team has "put the town on the map." In fact, Robinson has been picked by the sports writers throughout the state as the favorite to win the tournament title and become the state champions.

The head coach, however, faces a dilemma. The most outstanding player on the team who transferred to Robinson two years ago — the one whose performances have largely been responsible for the team's success — has been having considerable difficulty with math. The math teacher who teaches the class is also the head basketball coach.

The overall academic performance of the player has been marginal during the senior year. The poor performance in math has been consistent with the performance in all class work. The final math test taken during the week prior to the state tournament resulted in a grade which reduces the player's average in math below that required to meet academic eligibility standards. In accordance with the rules of the state high school association, eligibility certificates must be filed weekly and be certified by the school principal.

The failure conditions have now been established, and the teacher-coach is confronted with a decision relative to grade reporting. The player is aware of the test results and the consequences that may follow. The teacher-coach is visited by the player's father, who is also a member of the school board. No pressure is applied. The father simply reviews the importance of the team's performance at the tournament and its importance to the school and town and to their future.

As the teacher-coach ponders the predicament, an awareness of his or her uncertain future employment and social status in the community and/or the enhancement of a state-wide reputation for success presents itself. Personal factors in the situation are important because the teacher-coach has a young family who depend upon a steady and consistent financial income for subsistence.

The teacher-coach has not yet recorded the grade report on the eligibility certificate form to be forwarded to the principal's office, although the report is due in a few hours.

Regardless of *what should have been* relative to conditions prior to the enrollment of the student in the coach's math class or to the prevention of the occurrence of the incident prior to this point, the fact is that the situation as described exists *now.*

Discussion Questions*

1. What are the primary elements in the incident that characterize it as an ethical one? (C)
2. What has been the relation of grades received in math to grades in other subjects for this student? Does this indicate a consistently honest reporting of the teacher-coach? Would this practice of reporting in such a manner indicate anything significant about the character of the teacher-coach? (C)
3. How often must academic eligibility reports be submitted? What are the purposes of such reports? Why should the school be concerned about the maintenance of academic eligibility standards as a qualification for athletic participation? (C)
4. Is it possible to separate the two functions of the teacher-coach, that is, as a teacher responsible for the academic progress of the student and as a coach responsible for the athletic performances of the athlete? (C)
5. Do teachers who coach athletics confront problems with students which are different than those found by non-coaching teachers? (C)
6. Are teacher-coaches apt to yield to the pressures generated by people in their communities to win and thereby relinquish some of the time and responsibility needed to perform well as teachers in the classroom? How do you account for this, if true? (C)
7. How much prestige and improvement of financial conditions could the teacher-coach make as a result of falsifying the grade report? (C)

*The letters C, V, R, D, which appear at the end of each question are related to the four elements of an ethical incident. See Figure 9 and pp. 157-162.

8. How do you define prestige for a teacher-coach in terms of winning in this described situation? (C)
9. What is the role of the student-athlete in the context of this situation? Would you expect the student to speak out in defense of the academic performance or in admittance of a poor performance? (C)
10. Suppose you were the teacher-coach who had worked so hard to bring the team to such a high level of performance. What would be your tendency relative to a report following the visit of the student's father? (V)
11. If you decide to falsify the report, would you feel relieved to think that no one would know of your decision except the student and the student's father? (V)
12. To what extent can the teacher-coach be guided by the code of ethics established in the professions of teaching and coaching? (See code samples in Chap. 6.) (V)
13. How conscious do you think the teacher-coach would be of a code of ethics prescribed by professional educational organizations such as the N.E.A., the A.I.A.W., or the state high school athletic association? (V)
14. What possible courses of action are available to the teacher-coach in handling the situation? Place them in order from one extreme to the other. (V-R)
15. Suppose you, as the teacher-coach, decide to place the student into a position of ineligibility. List all the likely consequences that might result from the action. (V)
16. Suppose you, as the teacher-coach, decide to report the student's performance so as to keep him academically eligible for the tournament. List all the likely consequences that might result from the action (not in terms of the team's performance but the immediate and long-range effects on the teacher-coach and the student). (V)
17. Which of the possible alternatives seem most reasonable in terms of the greatest possible good or least possible harm to all persons concerned? (R)
18. Which of the possible alternatives seem least reasonable? (R)
19. Would the good that is derived by the entire school and

community because of the successful participation of the team in this tournament outweigh any question of wrong decision by the coach? After all, the coach as an individual will be gone someday, but the achievement of the team and its relation to the school will be forever recorded in the state high school athletic history. (R)

20. Suppose the team, even with its outstanding performer, does not win in the tournament? Isn't this possibility always present? Would it seem that efforts to retain the student's eligibility under the circumstances be in vain? (R)

21. What injustices may be involved wherein the student would be accorded special privileges in the way of re-tests or make-up tests, without at the same time affording the same privileges to all math students? (R)

22. Make a final judgment as to which alternative you would choose. On what ethical grounds related to the education and/or welfare of persons do you feel your judgment is correct? (D)

23. What are your feelings when your choice of decision is extended to include all humankind in situations that are the same or similar? (D)

24. What kind of substantive ethical support can you provide to strengthen the decision you have made? Reference to the content of the selected ethical systems presented in Chapter 3 may assist you. Are there other sources to which you might refer for support of your decision? (D)

25. Based upon the experience which you have had in considering and answering the questions presented in this ethical incident, develop at least one ethical principle that has intrinsic ethical validity. You might find it useful to refer to the introductory section on Clarification of Concepts Prior to Considering The Specific Ethical Incident as a supplementary source of assistance. (p. 169.)

DISCUSSION TOPICS AND ETHICAL INCIDENTS

The following ethical incidents are offered to serve as examples of realistic events which have occurred and continue to occur in physical education and sport. The incidents may be further described or reference may be made to many types of media to seek other kinds of incidents. The purpose here is to provide a working base for the ethical reasoning experience. The incidents should be placed into the Model in Figure 10 and subjected to discussion questions represented in the four phases of the reasoning experience. The ethical incidents are as follows:

A. Sherri Morgantheau was a teacher of physical education in a high school which was located in a rural area about fifty miles from a large metropolitan city. She had, as a child, participated in a program of postural exercises and dance as a means of developing grace of movement and improved cultural qualities. She had enjoyed a highly satisfactory experience in sports in high school. Upon entering college, she decided to major in physical education in preparation for a career in teaching and coaching. Because of her earlier training, she was quite adept at modeling and, during her period of teaching and coaching in the high school, took occasional assignments as a model on weekends in the city. These assignments provided a means of supplementing her income received from teaching.

Through contacts of a business nature, she contracted to pose as a nude for a center page illustration in *MEN* magazine, a photo which was later selected for publication. One of the parents in the high school community who was also a member of the high school board called the attention of the members of the board to the publication and the photo of Sherri. Somewhat shocked, the board requested an explanation from Sherri and then released her from her employment with the school. Their reasons for the dismissal were that a teacher in projecting pornographic images before the general public destroyed the ideals and principles on which education for good citizenship was based and that such actions were contrary to the stated goals and objectives of education. Sherri countered with the claim that there existed a distinct separation between her responsibilities as a teacher and the pursuits of the personal life, that she effectively fulfilled her duties as a teacher, and that judgment should be restricted to that phase of her life to which judgment related.

B. Tom Vidal is a professional football player who is also a homosexual. He readily admits that his coming to terms with his emotions and physical preferences for men was not an easy one. His entire life was absorbed with football and his record of achievement in the sport was most notable (captain of his high school team and all-state, captain of his college Rose Bowl team, and All-American). He found it difficult to reconcile the conflict between the concepts of a football player representing an impressive ideal of maleness whose success is predicated on bulk and blunt aggression and that of a homosexual as being effeminate. His admission of his preference for male lovers exposed him to the abuse of rigid, authoritarian coaches and teammates who were brutal in their teasing.

Since his whole life was highly dedicated to football, which he played with immense success, he turned to the occupation of coaching when his playing career ended. His homosexuality was, by then, well known. All his efforts to secure employment in coaching-teaching were unproductive. All his inquiries and applications went unanswered.

C. The physical education student is assigned for student teaching to a high school where paddling students is frequently used as a disciplinary measure. It is not the nature of the student-teacher to administer corporal punishment. The student-teacher anticipates that on an early occasion a request will be made by the regular teacher to "lay it on" some student who has demonstrated unacceptable behavior according to the rules of the physical education department. The student-teacher realizes that if there is a refusal to lay on the paddle (whose dimensions are 9 x 1 1/2 x 16 inches with a handle 4 x 1 1/2 x 18 inches), the resulting and final grade for the semester of student teaching will be low.

D. The coach, at the start of basketball practice, required all players to sign a contract of agreement. The contract stated that should any players be guilty of breaking the established training rules (drinking, smoking, late hours) they would be suspended from the team. It was believed that the coach administered the contract procedure so as to stress a stronger bond or commitment to the team and training. The season that followed was highly successful. Just prior to the start of the regional tournament to qualify for the state championships, the coach received a telephone call from one of the player's parents. The call reported a party in progress at the home of one of the students. The coach visited the party, observed a number of the players drinking, and suspended them immediately. The suspension affected most of the first-string players. Those remaining players who had not attended the party represented the school in the tournament but fared poorly. The coach's coaching contract was not renewed the next year.

E. It has been estimated that as many as 1000 foreign athletes from as far away as Australia, Sweden, Kenya, and Japan are competing on scholarships in the United States, including about 400 in track and field. Their importance on the outcome of college sports events and in the absorption of scholarship funds for athletes has been significant. For example, in one national track and field championships competition, foreign competitors won nine out of fifteen individual events and accounted for 40 percent of the total meet points. They also figure prominently in national soccer, hockey, and tennis tournaments. Many coaches and others have expressed concern. "How can you expect," asked one coach, "a nineteen-year-old freshman out of high school to compete on a comparable basis against a twenty-five-year-old freshman who has extensive experience in international competition?" Other coaches have stated that, because of special circumstances, they can't win without the international athletes (location of school, lack of area talent in a sport, etc.). The foreigners, they state, bring in new concepts on training and improve the knowledge and competitive levels of Americans. They also add a distinct cultural flavor to a team and a school. An opposing view states that the foreign athletes are recruited for the sole purpose of winning for a school and only on the pretext of aiding them to achieve educational objectives. Such practices deprive many worthy and financially deprived American students of achieving a college education.

F. Recently there has been evidence of agents who represent professional sports infiltrating high schools, especially in the big cities, as a means of establishing an early contact with future potentially successful athletes. A prominent coach who has observed the action describes a typical occurrence as follows: "An agent persuades an acquaintance (it could be a high school principal) to arrange a meeting with a top prep star. The three of them get together and the principal or acquaintance tells the student, 'This man is an attorney. He wants nothing from you. But he admires you as a player. All he wants to do is watch over your career and then, when the time comes, to handle your business affairs.'"

The important point that has been made is that, although the time for negotiating a professional contract is some years away, the agent has made a contact. The concept of early recruiting is considered to be a practice which may pay off at a later date. The contact with the student is maintained on a periodic basis by taking the athlete to an occasional dinner or to a professional sports event.

Opponents of the described practice indicate that the filtering of recruiting techniques from the professional ranks to the college down to the high school changes in the minds of students the concept of what participation in sport in educational institutions is intended; it distorts the true purposes of education and the role of sports in it; and it represents a disturbing influence on the minds of young people by presenting expectations which may never be realized. On the other hand, the practice places the relationship on a business basis, which is realistic in life and is no different than the process of preparing young people of talent and aptitude for a career.

G. Team A, during the regional basketball championships, scored a basket immediately after the half-time buzzer sounded. The points which were disallowed were counted by the official scorekeeper and were not removed from the scoreboard. The score at that point, counting the scored after-buzzer basket, was 38 to 32. The game ended with the score at 67 to 66 with team A the winner.

Team B filed a protest with the state high school athletic

association. The protest was considered by the executive secretary of the SHSAA and a hearing officer, in accordance with the rules of the association, and was rejected. Team B then filed a suit against the SHSAA in circuit court for an injunction against the association, asking for a decision of reversal of the loss of the game on the basis of the scorekeeper's error.

The circuit court upheld the protest and ordered the last half of the game to be replayed starting with the score at 38 to 32, just where it was when the first half ended.

Three types of expressions about the situation were made: (1) Membership in the SHSAA is voluntary, and such membership obligates schools to abide by its rules until such rules are changed through regular established procedures. For example, a game score is final as soon as the official signs the score book, even if later on injustice is thought to have been done. If the district court interferes with such process or similar processes in school basketball or any other sports administered by the association, and protest decisions end up in the courts, such actions would signal the end of school sports. (2) Protests, no matter to what extent they may be made, excluding violence, are legitimate in obviously error-made situations because the team and its players should take precedence over an organization such as the SHSAA. If one wants to gain the respect of the players, the school, and community, one must fight for them and their rights. (3) The outcome of sport events should be decided within the contest of the game (players, officials). Players should be big enough to take in stride the outcomes of such events even when such outcomes may represent disappointment.

H. It is the last half of the ninth inning. The score is 6 to 5 in favor of the team in the field. The team at bat has runners on second and third base with two out. The batter lines the ball to center field. The center fielder must come in fast to attempt a shoe-string catch but actually just traps the ball. The umpire is uncertain. As the fielder holds the ball in the glove high overhead as an indication of having caught it, the umpire rules it an out. The game is over and the visiting team wins. When questioned later as to whether the ball was really caught or trapped, the player says, "That's for the official to say, because that's the official's job."

I. Jefferson College is located in the suburbs of a medium-sized city and in a predominately white (Caucasian) environment. A large portion of the financial support for athletic teams comes from the local people. There is a high degree of interest in the basketball team. The team maintains several black players, some of whom are superior performers. A nucleus of the local sports enthusiasts who are substantial supporters of the team make it evident to the coach that they prefer the white players to play most of the time throughout the season. The coach decides to carefully consider this type of expression before giving a final reply as to what the decision will be.

J. The basketball game between two very prominent college teams ended in an intensive fight between the players. Several players were injured, while one was critically hurt. Team A, which was publicly indicted for having caused the difficulties, maintained a coach who had a reputation for showmanship, stingy defense, and a winning record. The coach placed winning above all else. Before the coach was employed, the team had not won a conference title for thirty years. Student and local interest had been very low. This coach was the fourth in five years, a situation which represented an effort to secure a winner. The coach, immediately upon being hired, had recruited three very talented players and developed a pre-game Harlem Globetrotters' type of warm-up routine which hyped-up the team and the local fans. By the end of the warm-ups and before the start of this particular game, the team and a capacity crowd were motivated to a point of frenzy. The game had been well officiated until the final thirty-six seconds. Team A had employed tactics which were clearly seen to be antagonistic and unethical, involving punching, kicking, and spitting. One player of team A, who had fouled out before the fight started, jumped off the bench, rushed on to the playing floor, and joined in the fight. Two players of team A were suspended as a result of the incident.

K. Following the completion of the Olympic Games, a series of accounts were published related to the practice of athletes in improving physical performances through means other than regularly recognized and acceptable training standards. Such practices included, among others, the use of muscle-building anabolic steroids, blood boosting (withdrawing and reinjection of either whole blood or packed red blood cells prior to competition), and muscle stimulation through induced electrical currents. The purposes of such measures were to increase muscular power and muscular strength for events which require these qualities and to increase cardiovascular efficiency and muscle endurance in order to improve the oxygen-carrying capacity of the blood. Although it is illegal to use drugs or take measures to seek advantage over others in athletic competitions, such practices have been evident. When such practices exist under conditions of disapproval, they have been termed unethical. Proponents of the practices have indicated that the political and prestige values which result from winning in international competition are worth the cost.

L. The so-called "ball tosser" in physical education is not an unfamiliar sight. The characterization is reserved for those teachers who neglect their teaching in order to devote their time and attention to other responsibilities or who, due to personal defects and lack of professional pride, disregard assigned tasks. They neither keep up to date on the most recent teaching methods nor remain professionally active. Their physical education programs for a four-year period (or for eternity) for college are indicated by touch football or field hockey in the fall, basketball in the winter, and softball in the spring.

The teacher of physical education who is also the head coach of a varsity sport tosses the single ball into the class of fifty-five students and then departs for the side-room office to continue working on the plays for Friday's big game. Student leaders are instructed to carry on the conduct of the class. Some students will play a basketball game, some will just goof off, while some will lie on the stage or mats and doze off.

M. The sectional basketball tournament for seventh and eighth grade teams was on hand. Qualifications for team membership included body weight, since the competition was known as a lightweight tournament. One particular team had two players who were cousins; one was a starting guard, the other a starting forward. One of them was sick with the flu at weigh-in time, which was the final check-in point for participation in the tournament. The coach approached the healthy student after weigh-in and instructed the player to be reweighed and to inform the weighers that the name was Sinkewicz. The assumption of the weighers would be, the coach stated, that since the player had already weighed in, this student was the cousin. Then, the coach indicated, if the sick Sinkewicz recovered before the tournament started, the player could enter. The coach stated that this wouldn't be lying because the weighers would simply be assuming too much.

N. It was announced to all junior high school students who reported for basketball tryouts that the best twelve would comprise the varsity squad. The student-teacher, who also served as the assistant coach, was taken aside by the head coach and told that the squad must not consist of twelve black players even if they proved to be the best. It was important, the coach stated, to maintain a representation of white players so as to placate the local community people and parents.

Chapter 6

PROFESSIONS AND THEIR
CODES OF ETHICS

 THE emergence of professions out of the development of vocations is a distinctive feature of modern Western history and society. There has been, of recent times, considerable forces operating in a changing culture which have exerted influences on the traditional concept of the role and functions of professions. This is particularly so in those professions that are genuinely humanistic in nature, with special reference to teaching and coaching. One needs to view the traditional ideals and goals of professionals in general as they are tempered by the forces of change in present-day culture and societal thinking.

Public criticisms leveled against professions are often based upon what is seen in the clash between the role of the individual in the context of personal freedoms and human rights (which support social functions for which the profession assumes central responsibility) versus the imposition of restrictions from external sources which attempt to limit those freedoms and rights. Members of professions are often confronted with the desire to adhere to their professional codes, while at the same time having to contend with rapid changes in the economic, social, and political pressures of the times.

The sections of the text that follow present the basic, traditional principles and characteristics of professions. However, they also interpret questions and evaluate the status and functions of some professions in our society at the present time.

WHAT IS A PROFESSION?

A profession is represented by a classification of persons who bring to their fellow·humans a service which is characterized by specialized skills, supported by a body of knowledge or intellectual theory, and highly motivated by the ideal of selflessness in improving the condition of humankind.

The concept of a profession exceeds the characteristics of a skilled service — the practice of a definite technique founded upon a specialized training. A closer examination of the criteria which qualifies a group to identify themselves as a profession goes beyond skills, techniques, or service.

The rapid expansion of knowledge in the basic and applied sciences and the acceleration of new developments in technology have led to the creation and growth of a large number of component fields. The personnel of these fields may be characterized as specialists who required preciseness in training, employ highly sophisticated techniques, and yield a specialized skill service based upon this training. But these component fields do not necessarily qualify as meeting the criteria for professions. Often their specialized technological skills represent a feeding back of the product of their skills to the total complex or content out of which they arose and to which they remain as integral parts with expectations of such a feedback. This type of function or service does not fit into the concept of a profession whose service role is entirely different, nor is it the banding together of practitioners moved by the recognition of common interests in an attempt to form a union or organization.

It is of some interest to note that the history of the evolution of professions has been characterized by self-examination of constituent memberships as to whether or not, and to what degree, the organization may qualify as a profession. Self-examination has been very helpful to such groups and has led to some changes in occupations that were once nonprofessional so as to evolve into full professional status.

What, then, characterizes a profession and a trade or technical field? A trade or technical field is indicated not because it employs tools or instruments or manual labor in the pursuit of its tasks. Many professionals also utilize tools and instruments, and they also engage in physical activity or manual work. Professionals and technicians do not derive their essential character from this criterion.

One of the chief distinguishing marks of the technician is that he or she employs rule-of-thumb procedures or routine skills which are not subjected to theoretical analysis nor modified by theoretical conclusions from that analysis. The professional employs principles or concepts which evolve from a theoretical frame of reference based upon an academic discipline or disciplines. A technician may engage in complex tasks, but these are largely performed through routine skills and follow specific rules. They operate in the absence of principles related to theoretical knowledge.

The technician does not need to apply a knowledge of principles based upon changing circumstances which require adaptations in judgment nor an interpretation of the basic principles which underlie routine performances. The carpenter, plumber, and the electrician, among others, perform tasks unrelated to the theoretical nature of the principles which evolve out of such disciplines as physics, engineering, chemistry, physiology, microbiology, etc., and with regard for the interrelationship between such disciplines.

Professionals must not only employ a theoretical analysis to tasks but must place the interrelationship between intellectual disciplines into a broader context of the life of humans and institutions.

ARE TEACHERS OF PHYSICAL EDUCATION AND COACHES OF COMPETITIVE SPORTS PROFESSIONALS OR TECHNICIANS?

The answer to this question lies in the manner and degree to which such personnel meet the criteria which has been established to assist in forming such a judgment. The vast majority of physical education teachers and coaches are transmitters of physical skills. It is through the teaching of skills and techniques that these personnel seek to achieve purposes which the successful learning of skills makes possible. It would seem, therefore, that several factors would need to be identified in order to arrive at a judgment as to whether teachers and coaches are professionals or technicians.

If it is true that persons often form judgments on the basis of what they see, they would no doubt, classify teachers of physical education and coaches engaged in teaching skills as technicians. The general public and others in the educational environment do not readily understand the underlying support which teaching and coaching receives from a body of knowledge or intellectual theory which may be brought to bear upon the teaching of specialized skills. Others observe only the skill-teaching aspect of what seems to be an entirely overt process.

After all, doesn't the teaching of such skills in games such as volleyball, basketball, gymnastics, dance, swimming, tennis, football, field hockey, golf, soccer, wrestling, fencing, softball, baseball, track and field, etc., require only the services of a technician? What else could possibly be involved? And doesn't the coach of competitive sports teach the skills and techniques as well as the strategies of the game to achieve only the purpose of winning? Of course, there is the human element involved; it may be conceded that teachers and coaches are generally people of a selfless nature, and many are dedicated to a commitment to human values above income, power, and prestige. That there are exceptions, just as there are in all human endeavors, is also conceded.

Not all physical educators are teachers of the physical skills embraced in sports and games, in movement education, in other basic skills essential as a foundation for later learnings, or in specialized skills for special populations. Some extend their educational preparation so as to enter graduate teaching and perform research. Some enter alternative or related careers whose basis of function is related to skill learning and teaching.

The answers to the questions that have been presented lie in the application of a set of criteria to form correct judgments. These criteria or, in another form, these characteristics of a profession are presented in the following section.

CHARACTERISTICS OF A PROFESSION

A profession is indicated by meeting, at least, the following six criteria:

1. An organized body of intellectual theory constantly expanded through continuous study and research.
2. An intellectual technique which serves as a base for theoretical analysis and is used to modify theoretical conclusions derived from that analysis.
3. An application of the technique to the needs of people.
4. A period of long training and/or educational preparation involving a comprehensive mastery in breadth and depth of knowledge and skills which are necessary to the successful application of services.
5. An association of the members of the profession into a closely knit group with a high quality of communication between them.
6. A code of ethics involving a structured series of standards which provide direction for conduct and are developed by and for its clientele, sometimes, but often not, with sanctions for enforcement.

Each of these characteristics will be examined in detail, with reference to the profession of physical education and sport as follows:

1. *An organized body of intellectual theory constantly expanded through continuous study and research.* This characteristic identifies professions as being primarily intellectual in nature. It supports the characteristic which provides for an intellectual technique or method, inasmuch as it pertains to a formal body of knowledge identified as an academic discipline, and forms the foundation of knowledge upon which technique is based.

Whitehead[42] has pointed out that an essential component of a profession is the performance of theoretical analysis of the activities of the profession in order to better adapt activities to the attainment of the purposes of the profession. This statement has direct relevance to the tasks of the physical educator and coach of competitive sports. Whitehead demonstrated that theoretical analysis must be based on an understanding of the nature of the activities so that the results of action can be foreseen. Thus, he said, "Foresight based upon theory, and theory based on understanding of the nature of things are essential to the profession" (p. 72). We would add to the need for understanding the nature of activities, the need for understanding the nature of people as they exist as individual persons and as they exist interpersonally. This is true because the basic materials with which the physical educator and coach works are people. The knowledge of persons is most essential.

The subject matter areas which comprise the organized body of intellectual theory in physical education and sport must be defined. The first classification of disciplines consists of the *basic* sciences of human anatomy, human physiology, physics with emphasis on mechanical principles, psychology with emphasis on personal and interpersonal relations, and sociology. Dependent upon the degrees of relevancies, options may be cited in the knowledges of physiological chemistry, mathematics — including basic statistics — and physical or social anthropology.

The second classification of intellectual disciplines are those which provide for a direct application of basic knowledges acquired in the basic sciences, that is, as the knowledges may be applied by the professional person in the teaching of physical education and coaching of competitive sports. These subject matter disciplines correspond to the basic knowledge areas and are indicated as kinesiology and mechanical analysis of movement, effects of exercise or physical activity on the physiological functions of the human organism, motor learning and/or behavior, and the psychology and sociology of physical education and sport.

The body of knowledge of intellectual theory essential to the physical educator and coach of competitive sports can, therefore, be structured into a three-dimensional thrust: (1) the study of the human being in a contextual environment called physical education and sport with influence as to how the setting affects the person, with particular emphasis upon the physical-psychological effects upon the individual(s), and embracing subareas of exercise science, human movement sciences, and psychological analysis of inner cognitive processes; (2) the study of a social institutional environment within which persons function and are influenced with reference as to how the persons affect the setting — with emphasis upon the history, philosophy, and sociology of and in physical education and sport; and (3) the synthesis and integration of knowledge which results from the study of the interrelationships of all components which comprise the contextual matrix of both physical education and sport with the person constituting the common denominator or central focus of attention.[33]

2. *An intellectual technique which serves as a base for theoretical analysis and is used to modify theoretical conclusions derived from that analysis.* This technique contrasts with one simply based on the customary way of doing things and modified only by trial and error.

The teacher or coach who employs the same techniques *as they were taught or coached* or who proceeds in a fashion so as to use that which works and discards that which fails has no chance of meeting the specifications of this criterion. The person who only copies the techniques from the winning coaches or effective teachers without regard for the application of theoretical analysis of the techniques will lack this hallmark of the professional. This means that, rather than employ the hit-or-miss method of teaching and coaching, the professional person, in addition to understanding the capabilities and limitations of persons, is also competent to create and adapt a system of techniques to fit both the individual and the process of interaction between individuals for the most effective performance.

The application of this criterion is appropriate for the conventional classroom, laboratory, physical skill learning area, or the competitive sports arena. It also means that the professional person bases the adaptation of techniques upon a background of knowledge gained in the foundational applied sciences of kinesiology and mechanical analysis or biomechanics, motor learning, physiology of exercise and physical activity, and anthromomentry, with its knowledge of human physique, and other sciences.

The work of Silvia,[34] who over a period of thirty-eight years developed and applied a substantive theoretical model for the

Figure 12. The erosion of personal and professional responsibility illustrated by the physical education ball tosser who neglects teaching to devote time and attention to other matters or who, by personal defects of laziness or lack of professional pride, disregards educational processes and objectives.

application of techniques to learn physical skills, serves as an excellent example of the application of this criterion. An integrated approach entitled the Hand-Foot Concept embraced six components for the effective application of intellectual techniques for theoretical analysis of skill learning: (1) cinematographical description and interpretation (use of moving film to describe mechanical and kinesiological principles of movement); (2) a neurological understanding underlying conscious control, including proprioception, exteroception, and motor control; (3) somatotyping with relation to personality traits; (4) myological analysis with emphasis on the prime movers; (5) a knowledge of articulations in types, axes of rotation, and actions; and (6) an understanding of mechanical principles of leverage, resolution of forces, and vector analysis.

3. *An application of the technique to the needs of people.* This characteristic is embraced within the concept of service to one's fellow within the specialized area identified within the profession. It means that within the profession there is a conscious recognition of a spirit of public service which places social duty as the highest goal of the profession. The attitude of the professional person is one of pride in service given rather than of interest in opportunity for personal profit.

The service motive, as an objective of professions, is a prominent one and serves as a means of assuring personal dedication to causes which are directly related to the education and/or welfare of people. It serves as a means of securing and furthering public confidence and trust in both professional personnel and the institutions which they serve as being capable of assuming moral responsibility and a moral consciousness for the welfare of those who require the services of professional groups. The tradition of service leads true professionals to place others whom they serve before their own interests and to give their utmost without regard to material awards.

The element which undermines and destroys the idea of service to others is selfishness, which is expressed in desires to make financial profits or gain power or prestige by using others in order to gain one's ends. Climbing or clawing over other people in order to get to the top of one's profession or occupation and then, having achieved a higher superior status, to suddenly become magnanimous is definitely not the mark of the professional person. The motive of securing money, power, or prestige must be subordinated to the ideal of enriching the lives of others by the unselfish giving of oneself through the highest developed abilities and talents of the profession, consistently meeting the needs of people and the public good.

In recent years the tradition of service as a characteristic of a profession has undergone some buffeting from several publics and from some in the professions of teaching and coaching. The efforts of teachers to improve the conditions for teaching so as to provide more benefits to students or to secure higher salaries when such salaries are of low subsistence levels are not to be construed as an abandonment of the ideal of service. Such efforts need not be interpreted as those motivated by selfish ends. The professional needs peace of mind and a freedom from forces which threaten one's livelihood. These factors, however, while of great importance and worthy of attainment, should not comprise the professional's prime preoccupation.

Coaches of competitive sports possess unlimited opportunities to be of humane service to youth. The ideal of service is often tested and relinquished under pressure of public ends, for the extrinsic goals of prestige, and, in some instances, for increased financial rewards. In such situations, the persons who should be the recipients of a type of professional service influenced by a moral responsibility and a moral consciousness for the welfare of others may be transformed into a means to be used for the selfish ends of the public or the coach.

4. *A period of long training and/or educational preparation involving a comprehensive mastery of breadth and depth of knowledges and skills which are necessary to the successful application of services.* This experience occurs prior to the entry into the profession. It involves provisions for acquiring substantive bodies of knowledge which issue from appropriate academic disciplines and which serve as a base for the theoretical analysis of skills and techniques. It also provides for a mastery of a broad variety of skills and techniques as a foundation for effective teaching, demonstration, and delivery of ser-

vices in the special field, be it in the classroom, laboratory, or clinical field of operation.

The extended period of educational preparation is to involve more than the knowledges and skills which pertain to the specialized field. The normal period of preparation for physical education personnel, whether it be for teaching in an educational setting such as a public or private school, in community or government agencies, or in private organizations, continues over the time required for the completion of the bachelor's degree. Within this period of time, other options may be available to the prospective professional in terms of subspecializations within physical education. These might consist of athletic coaching, athletic training, adapted physical education, aquatics, and prephysical therapy, among others.

Noncertificated programs may also be available which permit persons to prepare for nonpublic school positions and thereby omit meeting certification requirements established by state departments of education. Again, a person may elect to increase professional competencies by enrolling in graduate study at the master's and doctoral levels, depending upon the type and level of professional services desired.

A representative program of preparation of a physical educator who also possesses the competencies to coach competitive sports consists of the following six components, all of which, when properly integrated, may contribute toward the production of quality personnel for the profession:

a. *The program of general education or general studies.* This program may also be thought of as being synonymous with liberal education. There is a recognized need for a type of education for all persons, irrespective of their preparation for a professional specialization, which prepares them for effective living not only in a democratic culture but in the world at large. It is characterized by a nonspecialized and nonvocational learning which should be the common experience of all educated men and women. Such a program provides balance to a totally integrated educational program by off-setting tendencies to devote an undue amount of time to specialization. It recognizes the need for all persons entering the professions to secure some of the fundamental areas of human knowledge and an integrated view of human experiences that is essential both for personal balance and social wisdom.

People can too often acquire the competencies in a particular profession but fall short of a human wholeness and civic conscience which participation in family, community, national, and motivational affairs requires. The result of this component of educational preparation should provide persons with a means to a more abundant personal life and a stronger, freer social order.

A representation of the content areas of general education may include knowledge and understanding of (1) the organization and communication of ideas (English composition and speech, mathematics, and foreign languages); (2) the physical environment and biological inheritance (the basic physical and natural sciences of biology, chemistry, physics, geology, zoology, botany, etc.); (3) social inheritance and social responsibilities (social studies, history, geography, sociology, anthropology, government, etc.); (4) insights and appreciations (music, art, philosophy, literature, poetry, drama, logic, etc.); and (5) health and physical well being (physical education, recreation, leisure studies, and health education, etc.).

The elements included in this component are not unrelated to those elements in the program of specialization. For example, the humanities and the biological, physical, and social sciences enhance professional preparation. The basic sciences may form a foundation upon which a core of applied sciences basic to human movement and function may be developed. A mastery of the skills of effective communication for the clear expression of thoughts in speaking, writing, reading, and listening with understanding is important to professional personnel above the basic environment in association with others.

b. *The program of general professional education studies.* This program is so titled as to indicate those courses designed to provide for the elements which are common to all teachers whose professional services are offered in educational institutions, principally, public schools. This component may be by-passed in instances where there is no intention to enter public school teaching. Generally, this component provides a broad sweep of knowledge concerning the role of education in a democratic society and forms a basis for better understanding the role of the specialized offering in it. It also provides some general skills which are common to all teachers so as to produce a more effective educational climate for learning.

The primary thrust of this program is to meet legal certification requirements imposed by state departments of education, one of whose functions is to serve as a certification agency. Since states assume heavy financial responsibilities for the schools, they create conditions regarding the conduct of the schools. Among other matters, they establish requirements which must be fulfilled by those who teach in the schools. These requirements are frequently revised, and a variety of educational resources assist in the process. They maintain statutory powers to issue regulations respecting the professional competence or recognition of teachers. These measures provide minimum assurance of professional competency.

c. *The program of specialization for the profession.* This component of preparation for the profession occupies a major amount of time in the period of education of personnel. It is often referred to as the curriculum or program of professional preparation. It is subject to continual evaluation and often undergoes adjustment to meet changes which occur in the culture for which services are needed. Professional preparation is characterized not by a single structured curriculum for everyone but recognizes diversity in professional career planning and the shift in market trends within the total professional field.

The curriculum often is characterized by a core of knowledges and understandings which are considered to be essential to effective professional performance and which support a universally applied concept of human physical movement.

Because of its universality in application to all human movement, the core is also highly related to programs such as those identified as alternative career programs or satellite programs which revolve around and are highly related to physical education. The core consists of the physical, biological, and behavioral sciences in both their basic and applied forms, translated into meaningful understanding related to use in human movement and function; the core also consists of the sociocultural, historical, and philosophical aspects of movement and of the growth and development of the individual.*

The period of preparation also provides for the development of a personal proficiency in a wide variety of physical activity skill embraced in games, sports, exercise, and dance, together with a knowledge of methods and techniques of teaching these skills. Since physical education makes a considerable portion of its contribution to the individual and to society through the medium of human movement, such knowledges and abilities are imperative necessities for professional competence in this area of specialization.

Additionally, the period of preparation includes other elements, such as measurement and evaluation, as a means of establishing a scientific base for determining people's needs, program construction, teaching effectiveness, and the attainment of educational objectives; curriculum planning and organization; administration for conduct of programs; knowledge and skill to service special populations; and indicated needed competence in areas of highly related fields.

d. *The program of clinical experiences.* This component is commonly found in all programs of professional preparation. It assists in fulfilling that characteristic of a profession which indicates the need to possess skills and techniques as a means of offering one's services to others, fully supported by substantive knowledge which underlies the execution of the

---

*For a comprehensive treatment of this subject, reference may be made to the publication, *Professional Preparation In Dance, Physical Education, Recreation Education Safety Education, and School Health Education*, A.A.H.P.E.R., 1974. 1201 Sixteenth Street, N.W., Washington, D.C. 20036.

skills. The assigned clinical experiences represent a period of trial and practice for the prospective professional who performs under strict supervision. It is scheduled at a time when all prior and related competencies have been assured. If one intends to teach in a public school, the clinical experience is administered as a complete, integrated experience in teaching physical education and assisting in coaching competitive sports under qualified supervisors.

The entire clinical experience functions under a closely planned and coordinated program of guidance which is offered by the immediate supervisor and the university or college clinical experience supervisor. The primary intention of the clinical experience is to provide a realistic educational and practical experience in developing competency in the actual entrance into professional practice.

e. *The program of related professional experiences.* The provision of a curriculum for specialized professional preparation is not, in itself, considered sufficient for the production of competent personnel. The identification of competencies, either specifically or conceptually, invariably leads to the need for types of experience which the course curriculum cannot provide. If the major responsibilities of institutions which prepare physical education personnel is to design and provide varied experiences which will enable individuals to develop identified and recognized competencies for the profession, the role of related professional experiences outside of the curriculum becomes an important facet of the entire process.

While it is true that the quality of the faculty and their efficient application of a divergency in modes and models to facilitate learning are among the most critical factors in quality programs of professional preparation, it is also true that a supplement of either type of experiences is essential for the maximum development of the characteristics of a professional person in accordance with individual capacities and directions.

Some of these experiences are provided through membership, but particularly in leadership roles, in student professional organizations within the institution whose purpose is to provide a direct professional involvement. Other experiences may be provided through membership and personal action in professional associations external to the institution which provide for student interrelationships and functions; subscription to and reading of literature in current professional journals; writing for publications in the professional field; membership in intercollegiate and intramural athletic teams as participants, officials, managers, and athletic trainers; assisting in the testing and teaching process in basic instruction or service classes in physical education; participating as a member or leader in general campus programs of a service or humanitarian nature, such as the Special Olympics and Games and Sports for the Handicapped; assisting in the teaching and coaching of community youth groups and their programs sponsored by community agencies; and attending clinics, workshops, lectures, conventions, and conferences sponsored on campus, sectionally, state-wide, regionally, or nationally.

f. *The recruitment, selection, retention, and placement of prospective professional personnel.* These components of the total program of professional preparation provide assurance of a commitment of the institution to the profession of its concern for the educational preparation of high quality personnel; of an expression of a moral obligation to those human beings who will be the recipients of the services of the professional person; and, through a program of guidance, an equitable sense of justice to those who are excluded from the profession because of lack of qualifications.

Effective recruitment is based upon the coordination of the energy of several thrusts. These are (1) the reputation achieved by the institution in the area of specialized preparation for the specific profession (this reputation becomes known in a number of ways but principally by the quality of its product over a period of years); (2) the quality and reputation of an active faculty: The recruitment efforts of faculty are very helpful as they may be expressed in attendance at high school and community college career days, articulation conferences, and in clinics and workshops for prospective professionals; and (3) the use of alumni and institutional resources through personal contacts and through the dissemination of literature, conduct of career days, etc.

It is an important feature of programs of recruitment to provide objective information on admission policies and standards, objectives and content of the programs, and future market tendencies. It is also important that students be assisted in matching these data to their own aptitudes, expectations, and objectives.

The intensity of the criteria for the selection of personnel for specialization in the profession of physical education will depend upon the nature of the program demands, the standards established by the faculty of the special field, the objectives of the institution and the unit in which the special field resides, and often by the demands of the market. The level at which standards are established will often permit applicants to make individual decisions as to their own compatibility to meet the standards.

Some of the indicated prerequisites for success will include capabilities to master the intellectual content of general and special academic disciplinary offerings; a demonstrated ability of personal possession of a variety of physical skills with, perhaps, above average performance in at least one; a desire to offer professional services in a physical activity environment and a desire to work with and relate to people at all age levels; a desire to impart to others, through the ideals of service, a program of educational development through the avenues of physical education or human movement; a background of experience with children and youth in the physical activities of physical education; and evidence of leadership aptitude and ability. These criteria should apply at the point of application for admission from either high school or community college following proper articulation of programs.

The retention procedures will require periodic review of progress in meeting the established standards. This review will be coordinated so as to provide continual guidance and counseling procedures and thus provide optimum conditions for retention of personnel. Satisfactory progress toward meeting the standards or defined competencies most often will include the elements of academic records in terms of both grade point average and grade performance in individual courses; summaries of faculty responses pertaining to the evaluation of each individual as they relate to the standards; assessment of the present status of student goals; evaluation of activities and programs outside of the academic curriculum; guidance in assisting with personal problems; and, where the evidence merits it, encouragement and assistance to continue good or needed improvement in performance.

The placement services offered to professional personnel provides more than assistance to the task of finding employment. It aids in seeking a compatibility between the professional person and the future environment where services will be provided. Placement services provide the professional with a sense of belonging to a professional group of people who demonstrate an interest in his or her future career. It also helps to fulfill a moral commitment of the agency of professional preparation to both its own personnel and to its profession.

Placement services can be facilitated through coordination of efforts between the placement services of an institution and the faculty of the special field. Faculty should be sensitive throughout the year to a variety of opportunities for placement positions and, through personal involvement, assist in placement procedures.

5. *An association of the members of the profession into a closely knit group with a high quality of communication between them.* This type of relationship does not exclude the formation of subrelated groups within the association who maintain both their specialized identity and their parental organization association. Communication is typically effected through publication of scholarly journals, conferences, and conventions.

The common denominator which binds a closely knit group together with a professional identification is the opportunity for free association working in behalf of the purposes of the association and the recognized ideals of the profession. The desire to associate in the furtherance of these goals and the ability to do so are the prerequisites of an organization in a society which is free. When they do not wish to associate for common ends, they then have no vital purposes, because free association with freedom of communication is evidence of vitality and growth. If it is to be constructive as well as free, an association must be purposeful and its existence based upon the recognition of definite and well-recognized and accepted needs. It must make provisions for adjustments in its own nature and structure which are commensurate with the culture in which it exists and serves. If the association meets these general conditions, it will then exert a stabilizing influence upon its own profession and thus upon the society which it serves.

Persons desire to join an association for a variety of reasons. They may wish to place themselves into an environment which provides for a closer and enlarging contact with others so as to find an outlet and satisfaction for their own interests. They may wish to better express themselves and their ideas or, from a sense of obligation, to share with or contribute to others so as to add, even in a small way, some measure to the profession. An association of members in a profession enlarges its members' own view of what is taking place in the field, both in an immediate and specific sense and in the profession as a whole. It provides individual members with better opportunities for discerning and evaluating relationships between the many facets of the organization. It also provides a sense of camaraderie between members which creates a feeling of oneness and loyalty in purpose and aids in reinforcing one's philosphy of the worth of the profession and one's position in it.

Other types of benefits are also to be gained. These may include increased prestige and dignity among members for themselves and their groups and in the minds of the publics which they serve; some members exert political influence so as to preserve or improve their own status and become factors in political manipulation; some are effective in utilizing their collective source of strength for raising standards of financial renumeration for their group; and some become effective in influencing the thinking and acting of related groups, both governmental and private, through formal action expressed in statements of resolutions, platforms, pronouncements, etc., which carry greater weight on public opinion than when expressed by individuals.

It has often been charged that professions are nonprogressive in their attitudes toward the larger problems of social life, that they tend to make progress only in their own groove. In other words, professions tend to fail to see the relationships between the results of their deliberations to the problems of society at large; they fail to place their best efforts and thoughts into positions where society can best benefit. This charge implies that members in an organizational structure sometimes do not see the essential features of the social structure and the place of the professions in it. Moreover, members in a specialization do not interest themselves in the larger sphere of societal events or in matters outside their own special development of techniques and disciplines.

This charge has somewhat softened of recent dates because of (1) the increased relations between the theoretician and the practitioner and (2) the increased role of interaction between a variety of types of persons, all of whom function in a common profession with a greatly increased means of communication between them.

The primary point that is made by this charge is that it is essential that professions, by their very nature and purpose, see their functions as secondary in importance to the larger task of making more effective their special services so as to benefit society as a whole.

The structure of professional associations which permits the formation of subrelated groups within the association is evidenced in professions which have experienced the fragmentation of specialized groups. These groups maintain their specialized identification of their parental or umbrella-effect type of association. The tasks of the group, whether indicated as an association, federation, or alliance, are to provide a type of overall structure and supporting functions which permit each specialty to (1) maintain its own identity, (2) function with freedom within its own framework and toward common ends which are reflected in the services of a profession, and (3) have the freedom of communication within and between related specialized groups.

When those who wish to establish their own identities are deprived of these freedoms, they are most likely to depart from the larger unit and seek another attachment or establish their own independent structure.

The position of physical education and sport in members' professional structured and organizational status may be viewed relative to identity and relationship within the *American Alliance for Health, Physical Education, and Recreation.** The cohesive elements which bind together the subrelated groups within the Alliance are best expressed in the statements of purpose of the organization, which are as follows:

> Section 1. The alliance shall be an educational organization structured for the purposes of supporting, encouraging, and providing assistance to the member groups and their personnel throughout the nation as they seek to initiate, develop, and conduct programs in health, leisure, and movement-related activities for the enrichment of human life.

> Section 2. The general objectives to be sought in fulfilling the above stated purpose are:
> (1) Professional growth and development — to support, encourage, and provide guidance in the development and conduct of programs in health, leisure, and movement-related activities which are based upon the needs, interests, and inherent capacities of the individual in today's society.
> (2) Communication — to facilitate public and professional understanding and appreciation of the importance and value of health, leisure, and movement-related activities as they contribute toward human well-being.
> (3) Research — to encourage and facilitate research which will enrich the depth and scope of health, leisure, and movement-related activities; and to disseminate the findings to the profession and other interested and concerned publics.

---

*American Alliance for Health, Physical Education, and Recreation. Articles of incorporation. *Up-Date,* October 1974, p. 8.

(4) Standards and guidelines — to further the continuous development and evaluation of standards and/or guidelines within the profession for personnel and programs in health, leisure, and movement-related activities.

(5) Public affairs — to coordinate and administer a planned program of professional, public, and governmental relations that will improve education in the areas of health, leisure, and movement-related activities.

(6) To conduct such other activities as shall be approved by the Board of Governors and the Alliance Assembly. Provided that the Alliance shall not engage in any activity which would be inconsistent with the status of an educational and charitable organization as defined in Section 501 (c) (3) of the Internal Revenue Code of 1954 or any successor provision thereto, and none of the said purposes shall at any time be deemed or construed to be purposes other than the public benefit purposes and objectives consistent with such educational and charitable status.

The composition of organizational memberships within the Alliance who function in behalf of the stated purposes are the following:

AAHE — Association for the Advancement of Health Education.

AALR — American Association for Leisure and Recreation.

ARAPCS — Association for Research, Administration, Professional Councils, and Societies.

ASCSA — American School and Community Safety Association.

NAGWS — National Association for Girls and Women in Sport.

NASPE — National Association for Sport and Physical Education.

NDA — National Dance Association.

Other definable groups in physical education and sport have indicated other types of identification consistent with their own interests but which recognize theoretical and functional relationships between them. Personnel in higher education have expressed the need for an identification and grouping of specialists in various academic disciplines which could perform the purposes of seeking distinctiveness, of integrating and synthesizing knowledge from the academic disciplines and practices, and coordinating their services for use in service to practitioners.

Some suggested identified groups who experience such functions so as to suggest a central association, federation, or alliance are North American Society for Sport History, Philosophical Society for the Study of Sport, American College of Sports Medicine, North American Society for the Psychology of Sport and Physical Activity, and Anthropological Association for the Study of Play.

6. *A code of ethics involving a structured series of standards which provide direction for conduct and are developed by and for its clientele, sometimes but often not, with sanctions for enforcement.* A code of ethics as it pertains to a profession provides direction for one's behavior with particular reference to conduct within the confines of one's professional duties. However, an examination of the content of various codes reveals that the acceptance of the responsibility to adhere to the highest ethical standards involves, as well, one's personal conduct apart from the application of services within the profession. There continue to be differences of opinion and conflicting decisions on the points that (1) there should be a clear distinction between one's personal life conduct and the conduct exhibited in one's professional affairs, and (2) there needs to be a balance struck between the conflicting motives of egoism and altruism, that is, between a moral obligation to look out for one's self and his or her preservation and placing the higher value upon the welfare of others above material gain for oneself.

We shall examine in more detail the entire matter of codes of ethics in the section which follows. However, we may indicate that a scanning of a variety of codes of conduct for personnel in the professions are formulated so as to provide direction for human behavior in each of the six characteristics which comprise a profession. An examination of codes for the professions of teaching, medicine, law, physical therapy, engineering, business, nursing, dentistry, and others reveal as explicitly stated or implied a series of categories of treatment. These relate to such items as client welfare, professional autonomy, academic freedom and tenure, occupational competition, confidentiality, political action, altruistic aims, offering and withholding services, gifts and gratuities, relation with other organizations, commitment to employment practices, and collective bargaining.

The projection of ethics into the practices of physical education personnel has been made by Rarick, Massey, Johnson, Shea, and Frost. Their views present recommended practices in the classifications of (1) research, its accountability and conduct with human subjects; (2) teaching, with reference to its validity, integrity of purpose, ownership of student materials, confidentiality of student information, evaluation of students, and student-teacher relationships; (3) writing and publishing, with relation to the responsibilities of the individual author or writer; (4) relationships between administrators, teachers, and the publics; and (5) speaking and representing others in the transmission of ideas and ideals.*

CODES OF ETHICS IN PROFESSIONS

A profession's code of ethics commits its members to social values expressed in the improvement of the welfare of their fellow humans and provides direction as to how its members may seriously dedicate themselves to these values. The code makes a clear distinction between the altruistic type of behavior the professional person must possess and exhibit and the egoistic type of behavior which issues from selfish desires and motives to secure income, power, and prestige. Examples of the relation between high social values to be achieved by professional personnel and the nature of their professions are provided in various codes.

---

*A detailed and comprehensive treatment of these presentations apart from what is presented here will be found in *The Academy Papers*, Number 9, of the American Academy of Physical Education, October 1975. The excerpts have been adapted and reprinted with the permission of its publisher.

The code of ethics in medicine provides central direction for physicians toward saving and improving the lives of patients and promoting the healthful welfare of others above all material and personal gains. The ethical code for the teaching profession dedicates the teacher toward the pursuit of truth, the protection of freedom to learn and to teach within a context of educational opportunity for all, which supports the concept of the worth and dignity of persons. The established code of ethics for the clergy demonstrates the exceedingly high devotion of efforts in the service of God and in transmitting religious ideals to parishioners above all selfish consideration.

The codes of ethics for other professions, such as law, business, engineering, dentistry, ministry, nursing, or physical therapy, contain as their essential theme the subversion of personal and selfish interests to those of a high social order and social service to others whom they serve.

The development of codes of ethics is formulated and approved by the constituencies who are identified within each profession. They are periodically reviewed, reinterpreted, and reworded so as to comply with acceptable standards of behavior as such standards conform to the central theme of high social order and social service to others whom they serve. Just as values are subject to change and reinterpretation, standards within the codes change. This seems to be especially so as the values within a culture shift in emphasis between the relative status of the individual and his or her freedoms and that of the social group.

In recent years there has been a transition from earlier types of expressions of standards in their general, rather vague platitudes of statements of principles to more explicit, enforceable, and specific directives for conduct. This has been a result of the changing times from a permissive type of culture, which places high emphasis on material gains, into one which places more responsibility upon the individual in relation to one's accountability for acceptable professional competence. There has also been an influence of ethical relativism upon the formulation of judgments as to what constitutes right or wrong conduct within the context of existing circumstances.

For example, outside or supplemental employment might impair the professional effectiveness of the teacher, but he or she might still perform on an efficiency scale above the level of the person's colleagues. One might also ask, To what extent might the source of an individual's supplemental income have as an effect on one's status as a professional? That is, should there be a clear demarcation between one's personal activities apart from a person's professional responsibilities on the job and the possible effect such activities might have on one's professional status? One's engagement in political affairs affords an example of such an involvement, but suppose the teacher or coach poses for the center page in *Playboy*® magazine? Is what a person does in his or her personal affairs to be indicated in professional codes pertaining to professions?

There has also been an increase of conflicts in the position of some professions concerning the ideal of service to humankind and the selfish desires of the individual. The public, who are the recipients of the benefits of programs of education, often form their judgments of the status of professional personnel on the basis of what they see and what they read. Their observations of the behavior of personnel who are engaged in the highly ranked service professions, such as medicine and its related fields and teaching, among others, are subject to misinterpretation when the same type of activities are engaged in by personnel in nonprofessional occupations. Labor strikes and collective bargaining measures which are often viewed as selfish interest-motivated seem to conflict with what the public view as motives centered upon the education and welfare of children and youth.

A profession, irrespective of adjustments in the interpretation of its code based upon changes in the context of a culture, does establish some form of group discipline in support of the values which are expressed in the code. This action assumes as much as possible the suppression and elimination of selfishly motivated activities and programs. Group discipline based upon a general recognition and acceptance of the code by the membership is imposed to better uphold the ethical values to which the group dedicate themselves. The sanctions of discipline may be manifest through overt action taken by established measures such as disbarment of lawyers, rescinding of licenses to practice for physicians, public reprimand, and a rejection from membership in the group. In its mildest form, discipline may be expressed through the personal actions of members to ostracize the offender.

In the sense that a profession dedicates itself to high social values which benefit all humankind rather than more narrow interests of the group, it is not a union. It is particularly ironic in this light of comparison that in spite of the two basic criticisms of the need for separation of one's personal life from professional life and the conflict between the egoistic and altruistic motives that codes of ethics make their major contribution.

An awakening of the ethical consciousness on the part of professional groups in this country is evidenced in the hundreds of codes of ethics which have developed since the turn of the century. There is a greater consciousness in our national life today for the moral and ethical conduct of those in positions of economic, social, and political leadership. While it is impossible to present even a representative sampling of the large variety of codes in a text, a presentation is made of two which are very relevant to the teacher of physical education and sport. Each student of the ethical study experience should examine these codes and, after becoming familiar with their provisions, attempt to determine their merits and defects with reference to the ethical problems which arise in connection with their provisions. The two codes presented here will serve as guides for this type of practice.

MODEL CODES OF ETHICS

Code of Ethics of the Education Profession
Adopted by the 1975 NEA Representative Assembly

The educator, believing in the worth and dignity of each human being, recognizes the supreme importance of the pursuit of truth, devotion to excellence, and the nurture of democratic principles. Essential to these goals is the protection of freedom to learn and to teach and the guarantee of equal educational opportunity for all. The educator accepts the responsibility to adhere to the highest ethical standards.

The educator recognizes the magnitude of the responsibility inherent in the teaching process. The desire for the respect and confidence of one's colleagues, of students, of parents, and of the members of the community provides the incentive to attain and maintain the highest possible degree of ethical conduct. The Code of Ethics of the Education Profession indicates the aspiration of all educators and provides standards by which to judge conduct.

The remedies specified by the NEA and/or its affiliates for the violation of any provision of this Code shall be exclusive and no such provision shall be enforceable in any form other than one specifically designated by the NEA or its affiliates.

Principle I — Commitment to the Student

The educator strives to help each student realize his or her potential as a worthy and effective member of society. The educator therefore works to stimulate the spirit of inquiry, the acquisition of knowledge and understanding, and the thoughtful formulation of worthy goals.

In fulfillment of the obligation to the student, the educator —

1. Shall not unreasonably restrain the student from independent action in the pursuit of learning.
2. Shall not unreasonably deny the student access to varying points of view.
3. Shall not deliberately suppress or distort subject matter relevant to the student's progress.
4. Shall make reasonable effort to protect the student from conditions harmful to learning or to health and safety.
5. Shall not intentionally expose the student to embarrassment or disparagement.
6. Shall not on the basis of race, color, creed, sex, national origin, marital status, political or religious beliefs, family, social or cultural background, or sexual orientation, unfairly:
   a. Exclude any student from participation in any program.
   b. Deny benefits to any student.
   c. Grant any advantage to any student.
7. Shall not use professional relationships with students for private advantage.
8. Shall not disclose information about students obtained in the course of professional service, unless disclosure serves a compelling professional purpose or is required by law.

Principle II — Commitment to the Profession

The education profession is vested by the public with a trust and responsibility requiring the highest ideals of professional service.

In the belief that the quality of the services of the education profession directly influences the nation and its citizens, the educator shall exert every effort to raise professional standards, to promote a climate that encourages the exercise of professional judgment, to achieve conditions which attract persons worthy of the trust to careers in education, and to assist in preventing the practice of the profession by unqualified persons.

In fulfillment of the obligation to the profession, the educator —

1. Shall not in an application for a professional position deliberately make false statement or fail to disclose a material fact related to competency and qualifications.
2. Shall not misrepresent his/her professional qualifications.
3. Shall not assist entry into the profession of a person known to be unqualified in respect to character, education, or other relevant attribute.
4. Shall not knowingly make a false statement concerning the qualifications of a candidate for a professional position.
5. Shall not assist a noneducator in the unauthorized practice of teaching.
6. Shall not disclose information about colleagues obtained in the course of professional service unless disclosure serves a compelling professional purpose or is required by law.
7. Shall not knowingly make false or malicious statements about a colleague.
8. Shall not accept any gratuity, gift, or favor that might impair or appear to influence professional decisions or actions.

The Association For Intercollegiate Athletics For Women has published a Code of Ethics which, in content, is most comprehensive. It embraces subcodes for coaches, players, administrators, officials, and spectators. The purpose of the Code is to assist personnel and students to identify ethical conduct in intercollegiate sports and to pursue appropriate action which is guided by the Code provisions. The sections reproduced in this text are intended to be representative of the nature of the Code. The complete Code may be viewed through reference to the *AIAW Handbook*.

Association for Intercollegiate Athletics for Women Code of Ethics*

Ethical Considerations for the Coach

1. Respect each player as a special individual with unique needs and characteristics and develop this understanding and respect among the players.
2. Have pride in being a good example of a coach in appearance, conduct, language, and sportsmanship, and teach the players the importance of these standards.
3. Demonstrate and instill in players a respect for and courtesy toward opposing players, coaches and officials.
4. Express appreciation to the officials for their contribution and appropriately address officials regarding rule interpretations of officiating techniques. Respect their integrity and judgment.
5. Exhibit and develop in one's players the ability to accept defeat or victory gracefully without undue emotionalism.
6. Teach players to play within the spirit of the game and the letter of the rules.
7. Develop understanding among players, stressing a spirit of team play. Encourage qualities of self-discipline, cooperation, self-confidence, leadership, courtesy, honesty, initiative and fair play.
8. Provide for the welfare of the players by:
   a. Scheduling appropriate practice periods,
   b. Providing safe transportation,
   c. Scheduling appropriate numbers of practice and league games.
   d. Providing safe playing areas,
   e. Using good judgment before playing injured, fatigued, or emotionally upset players,
   f. Providing proper medical care and treatment.
9. Use a consistent and fair criteria in judging players and establishing standards for them.
10. Treat players with respect, equality, and courtesy.
11. Direct constructive criticism toward players in a positive, objective manner.
12. Compliment players honestly and avoid exploiting them for self-

---

*Reproduced with permission of the National Association for Girls and Women in Sport, *American Alliance for Health, Physical Education and Recreation*. 1201 Sixteenth Street, N.W., Washington, D.C. 20036.

glory.
13. Emphasize the ideals of sportsmanship and fair play in all competitive situations.
14. Maintain an uncompromising adherence to standards, rules, eligibility, conduct, etiquette, and attendance requirements. Teach players to understand these principles and adhere to them also.
15. Be knowledgeable in aspects of the sport to provide an appropriate level of achievement for her players. Have a goal of quality play and excellence. Know proper fundamentals, strategy, safety factors, training and conditioning principles, and an understanding of rules and officiating.
16. Attend workshops, clinics, classes, and institutes to keep abreast and informed of current trends and techniques of the sport.
17. Obtain membership and be of service in organizations and agencies which promote the sport and conduct competitive opportunities.
18. Use common sense and composure in meeting stressful situations and in establishing practice and game schedules which are appropriate and realistic in terms of demands on player's time and physical condition.
19. Conduct practice opportunities which provide appropriate preparation to allow the players to meet the competitive situation with confidence.
20. Require medical examinations for all players prior to the sports season and follow the medical recommendations for those players who have a history of medical problems or who have sustained an injury during the season.
21. Cooperate with administrative personnel in establishing and conducting a quality athletic program.
22. Accept opportunities to host events and conduct quality competition.
23. Contribute constructive suggestions to the governing association for promoting and organizing competitive experiences.
24. Show respect and appreciation for tournament personnel and offer assistance where appropriate.
25. Be present at all practices and competitions. Avoid letting other appointments interfere with the scheduled team time. Provide time to meet the needs of the individual players.
26. Encourage spectators to display conduct of respect and hospitality toward opponents and officials and to recognize good play and sportsmanship. When inappropriate crowd action occurs the

coach should assist in curtailing the crowd reactions.

Ethical Considerations for the Player:
1. Maintain personal habits which enhance healthful living.
2. Objectively acknowledge one's own strengths and weaknesses. Recognize that each person has his own strengths and weaknesses — praise the strengths and help to strengthen weaknesses.
3. Value one's personal integrity.
4. Respect differing points of view.
5. Strive for the highest degree of excellence.
6. Willfully abide by the spirit of the rules as well as the letter of the rules throughout all games and practices.
7. Uphold all standards and regulations expected of participants.
8. Treat all players, officials and coaches with respect and courtesy.
9. Accept victory or defeat without undue emotion.
10. Graciously accept constructive criticism.
11. Respect and accept the decisions of the coach. When ethical decisions are questionable, the participant should direct her questions to the coach in private and follow appropriate channels to voice her concerns.
12. Be willing to train in order to achieve one's full potential.
13. Respect the achievements of the opponent.
14. Extend appreciation to those who have made the contest possible.
15. Be grateful for the opportunity afforded by the intercollegiate program and be willing to assist in program tasks as evidence of this gratefulness.
16. Assist in promoting positive relations among all participants who are striving to achieve athletic excellence.
17. Exhibit dignity in manner and dress when representing one's school both on and off the court or playing field.
18. Respect the accomplishments of one's teammates.
19. Expect fans to treat officials, coaches and players with respect.
20. Recognize the value of the contribution of each team member.
21. Keep personal disagreements away from practices and contests.
22. Keep the importance of winning in perspective with regard to other objectives.
23. Contribute to the effort to make each practice a success.
24. Exert maximum effort in all games and practices.
25. Seek to know and understand one's teammates.
26. Place primary responsibility to the team rather than to self.
27. Refrain from partaking of drugs which would enhance perfor-

mance or modify mood or behavior at any time during a season unless prescribed by a physician for medical purposes.

28. Refrain from partaking of alcoholic beverages while representing one's school.

DISCUSSION TOPICS AND ETHICAL INCIDENTS

1. If both teachers of physical education and coaches of sports are transmitters of physical skills, wherein lie the differences relative to the definition of a professional and a technician? Should there be differences in the identity of these personnel? What are the factors which help to decide whether or not there are or could be differences? (pp. 184-185.)

2. What answers can you provide to the question, Since teachers of physical education and coaches of sports are principally transmitters of physical skills, why can't their formal preparation be performed in a technical school or college of professions? A concentrated preparation in a two-year program culminating in an Associate of Arts degree would seem sufficient to produce a competent specialist in skills teaching. (pp. 185-186.)

3. Why should a theoretical analysis of the nature of people as well as of activities be considered important as a characteristic of both teachers of physical education and coaches? (p. 188.)

4. What can you suggest that would represent ways for teachers of physical education or coaches to improve their effectiveness other than employing techniques as they themselves were taught or coached or in attending clinics and conferences to secure the techniques found workable by others? (p. 189.)

5. Based upon your personal observations and experiences, to what degree do you believe teachers of physical education and coaches of competitive sport possess and apply a conscious recognition of a spirit of public service which places social duty as the highest goal of their profession? How do *you* feel about this characteristic of the profession (social duty) of teaching and coaching as compared with the development and fostering of opportunities for personal gain, financial profit, power, or prestige? (p. 191.)

6. Teachers of physical education and coaches of sports have sometimes been accused of isolating themselves from other professional associates or of failing to participate in school and community civic affairs. If this might be true for them, as well as for members of other professions, what could be some of the reasons that they fail to interest themselves in the larger sphere of societal events or in matters which lie outside of their own special technique and discipline? (p. 202.)

7. What are some of the specific ways that a code of ethics can make its contribution to a profession in terms of aiding the profession to dedicate itself to high social values rather than to the narrow interests of the group? Examine the codes in this text pertaining to the NEA (teachers) and the AIAW (coaches). Are these ways reflected in the stated purposes of the codes? Indicate specifically how these values are expressed. (pp. 206-209.)

8. The ethical incidents which follow are directly related to the professional behavior of persons who occupy positions of educational leadership. Indicate and explain your judgment of the decisions made by the teachers and coaches in each incident. Do the decisions and actions represent examples of adherence to a professional code of ethics? Indicate and describe where there seem to exist inconsistencies with a code of ethics for teachers of physical education and coaches of sports in each of the incidents described.

A. The basketball coach is unhappy with the work of the officials because their decisions seemingly are disadvantageous to the coach's team. When the fans at a home game demonstrate their displeasure of the officials' calls, the coach purposely acts so as to secure a technical foul. The purpose is to further incite the fans against the officials in the hope of intimidating them.

B. It is a common rule among states to specify a starting date for high school football practice. Many schools disregard this rule by starting early. A particular school conducts practice sessions starting the week after school lets out for summer vacation. The practice sessions mainly consist of conditioning and what looks like simple touch football games without coaches being present. However, attendance is maintained and reported to the coaches. Pressure is exerted on the players to regularly report for this practice program.

C. It is a common practice in the sport of wrestling to "weigh-in" the contestants at a specified number of hours prior to the start of the competition. The establishment of weight classes for competition is intended to provide for an equality of distribution among all who compete in the sport. The weigh-in process is intended to provide for an equalization of conditions so as to prevent unfair weight advantages.

Coach Green advises two of his wrestlers who slightly exceed the weight limits in their classes at the time of weigh-in to place their feet on the forward part of the scale platform with the toes curled over the front edge and to lean forward slightly. This technique permits a downward fluctuation of the weight indicator.

D. Coaches frequently break or bend their own self-made rules when it is expeditious to do so.

The coach made it very clear before the season's practice started that there would be no toleration of breaking the rules. Either "shape up or ship out" was the way the coach phrased it. Among the rules stressed were tardiness, absences, smoking, and late hours. An infraction of any of these rules meant dismissal from the team and at the very least not playing in the game following the infraction of the rule. Prior to the next home game, which was the big homecoming event, the player without whom the game could not be won was late for practice. The coach announced that the player would not play in the game but would "sit on the bench." As the game progressed, the home team fell behind in scoring. Considerable pressure mounted to enter the penalized player in the game. After some hesitation, the coach entered the player.

E. A sensitive question in publishing materials, theses, or dissertations is that of authorship. In this instance, the chairperson of graduate students program and theses advisor consistently applies a practice of publishing student theses with the consent of the student, but always with the advisor's name in the primary position of authorship. The questions that arise are, Is this practice ethically acceptable? Under what conditions might it be acceptable? Under what conditions might it be unacceptable?

F. There is a college position available for which candidates must be capable of coaching the varsity basketball team and teaching kinesiology and biomechanics. The position represents a cross-appointment of 50 percent in the budgeted athletic department and a budgeted 50 percent in the department of physical education. Both departments are separate and autonomous. The applicants are clearly distinguished in one of the two areas but not in both. In which direction would you move in making a decision of selection of one of the candidates? If you were responsible for the quality of the physical education program, would you give in to pressures of the athletic director, public, alumni, and students to employ the basketball coach? If you were responsible for the quality of the athletic program, would you give in to the pressures of the academic unit to employ the kinesiology teacher? How can the dilemma be best resolved?

G. The rules of the state high school association and the particular high school league permitted wrestlers to be weighed in at home for away meets. However, the weigh-in must be conducted within two hours of the start of the meet. Prior to the dual meet between the teams striving for the league championship, the coach of one of the teams weighed in the wrestlers before school started on Friday morning, although the meet was not scheduled to start until 7:30 PM that evening. The extra hours prior to the meet allowed time to replenish the strength of those who had extended themselves over a period of time to cut weight to enter lower classes.

H. Mary Brown's base teaching salary was $9,000. She receives an additional $800 for coaching varsity basketball. She has been informed that she can expect a generous and substantial raise in salary because her team won the state tournament. Her reputation as a teacher is extremely low. She neglects teaching her physical education classes and has been characterized as a ball tosser (one who neglects teaching responsibilities in order to devote time and energies to other interests and duties). On the other hand, Susan Jones is not assigned to sport-coaching duties but is a conscientious and dedicated teacher who spends many out-of-school hours in class preparation, student counseling, and student projects. She will get her scheduled 4 percent raise in salary. Susan experiences personal and professional difficulty in reconciling the discrepancy in salary recognition.

I. The local high school needs a head football coach but has no teaching positions available. The school board arbitrarily creates the position of assistant principal in charge of student nonacademic affairs in order to secure the talents of a very prominent coach. Describe the ethical implications of such a decision and its effects on teachers and local taxpayers.

J. The financial reductions in school athletic budgets throughout the country during a period of high inflationary conditions and diminished incomes to support educational costs have often meant the elimination of sports programs. When the Rockport School Board decided to eliminate the sports program in the high schools of the city, it left many excellent boy and girl athletes without any opportunity to continue their participation (and excluding a possible extension of chances to secure college admission recognition). The Doran Central Catholic High School, a private school located in the city, was faced with the temptation of admitting many talented athletes as transfers from the public schools to their student body. But the coaches and administrators of the DCCHS decided against such a move, feeling that it wouldn't be fair to those students who had already worked so hard to gain a place for themselves in the Doran rigorous programs.

Consequently, it was made known to parents and athletes eager to enroll in Doran that there wouldn't be any room on the varsity squads.

K. Look carefully at the codes of the NEA and the AIAW if teaching and coaching are fields which you intend to enter. In what respects does the content of these codes indicate possibilities for ethical problems and decisions? Do the contents represent preventive provisions, that is, guides for a type of behavior which would offset unethical or unprofessional actions?

L. Identify some of the economic pressures which operate on teachers today, causing them to form unions, conduct collective bargaining, and go on strike. Are these behaviors justifiable in view of such economic conditions? How do you reconcile these behaviors with the teachers' code of ethics?

M. Do teachers abandon their stature as professional persons when they resist or speak out against governmental restrictions to their personal freedoms and human rights? Identify some of these restrictions that issue from the national and/or state governmental sources that influence teacher functions.

N. What are some of the conditions with which teachers of physical education must contend as a result of the liberalization of behavior and thinking today, as for example, the establishment of student rights and freedoms? Is discipline a problem that emerges from student behavior? How can a teacher handle disciplinary problems of students and still adhere to the expectations of a profession?

BIBLIOGRAPHY

1. Abelson, Raziel and Friguegnon, Marie-Louise: *Ethics for Modern Life.* New York, St. Martin, 1975.
2. Assocation for Intercollegiate Athletics for Women: *AIAW Handbook, 1976-1977.* Washington, D.C., American Alliance for Health, Physical Education, and Recreation, 1976.
3. Burns, J. H. and Hart, H. L. A. (Eds.): *An Introduction to the Principles of Morals and Legislation: Collected Works of Jeremy Bentham.* University of London, Athlone Pr. Humanities, 1970.
4. Casteel, J. D. and Stahl, R. J.: *Value Clarification in the Classroom: A Primer.* Pacific Palisades, Goodyear, 1975.
5. Dewey, John and Tufts, J. H.: *Ethics,* rev. ed. New York, Holt, 1932.
6. Dewey, John: *Reconstruction in Philosophy.* New York, HR&W, 1920.
7. Fagan, Clifford B.: Player brawls must be eliminated. *The Illinois Interscholastic, 48:*267, 1976.
8. Frost, Reuben B. and Sims, Edward J. (Eds.): *Development of Human Values Through Sports: Proceedings of a National Conference.* Washington, D.C., American Alliance of Health, Physical Education, and Recreation, 1974.
9. Garnett, A. Campbell: *Ethics: A Critical Introduction.* New York, Ronald, 1960.
10. Hegel, G. W. F.: *The Philosophy of Right.* Translated by T. M. Knox. Oxford, Clarendon, 1942.
11. Hill, Thomas E.: *Ethics in Theory and Practice.* New York, CCPr. MacMillan, 1956.
12. Hobbes, Thomas: *The Metaphysical System of Hobbes,* with extracts from *Leviathan,* selected by Mary Whiton Calkins, 2nd ed. La Salle, Ill., Open Court, 1948.
13. Ignizio, J. P. and Gupta, J. N.: *Operations Research in Decision Making.* New York, Crane-Russak Co., 1975.
14. James, William: *Principles of Psychology.* New York, HR&W, 1923.
15. Kant, Immanuel: *Foundations of the Metaphysics of Morals.* Indianapolis, Bobbs, 1959.
16. Kissinger, Henry A.: *A World Restored.* Boston, HM, 1957.
17. Kohlberg, Lawrence: The cognitive-developmental approach to moral education. *Phi Delta Kappan, 56:*670-677, June 1975.
18. Landers, Daniel M. (Ed.): *Social Problems in Athletics: Essays in the Sociology of Sport.* Urbana, U of Ill Pr, 1976.

221

19. Leonard, George Burr: *The Ultimate Athlete: Revisioning Sports, Physical Education and the Body*. New York, Viking Pr, 1975.
20. Lillie, William: *An Introduction to Ethics*. New York, B & N, 1961.
21. McGlynn, George H.: *Issues in Physical Education and Sports*. Palo Alto, Calif., Natl Press, 1974.
22. Mitchell, Edwin T.: *A System of Ethics*. New York, Scribner, 1950.
23. Mortimer, R. C.: *The Elements of Moral Theology*. New York, Har-Row, 1947.
24. Munitz, M. K. (Ed.): *A Modern Introduction to Ethics*. Glencoe, Free Press, 1958.
25. Neal, Patsy and Tutko, Thomas A.: *Coaching Girls and Women: Psychological Perspectives*. Boston, Allyn, 1975.
26. Nietzsche, Friedrich: *Beyond Good and Evil*. Translated by Marianne Cowan. Chicago, Gateway Editions, Regnery, 1955.
27. Osterhoudt, Robert G.: *The Philosophy of Sport: A Collection of Original Essays*. Springfield, Thomas, 1973.
28. Patterson, Charles H.: *Moral Standards: An Introduction to Ethics*. New York, Ronald, 1957.
29. Pepper, Stephen C.: *Ethics*. New York, Appleton-Century-Crofts, 1960.
30. Raths, L. E., Harmin, M., and Simon, S. B.: *Values and Teaching: Working With Values in the Classroom*. Columbus, Ohio, Merrill, 1966.
31. Ross, Stephen D.: *The Nature of Moral Responsibility*. Detroit, Wayne St U Pr, 1973.
32. Royce, Josiah: *The Philosophy of Loyalty*. New York, Macmillan, 1916.
33. Shea, Edward J.: Sport as a theoretical base for physical education. *The Academy Papers*. The American Academy of Physical Education, 7:16-17, 1973.
34. Silvia, Charles A.: *Manual and Lesson Plans for Basic Swimming, Lifesaving, Water Stunts, Springboard Diving, Skin and Scuba Diving, and Methods of Teaching*. Springfield, Mass., Privately published by the author, 1970.
35. Slusher, Howard S.: *Man, Sports, and Existence: A Critical Analysis*. Philadelphia, Lea & Febiger, 1967.
36. Stace, W. T.: *The Concept of Morals*. New York, Macmillan, 1962.
37. Stahl, Robert J.: *Values and Moral Education: A Synthetic Model*. Washington, D.C., ERIC Clearinghouse on Education, 1976.
38. Titus, Harold H.: *Living Issues in Philosophy*, 3rd ed. New York, American Book Co., 1959.
39. Titus, Harold H. and Keeton, Morris: *Ethics for Today*, 5th ed. New York, Van NosReinhold, 1973.
40. Tutko, Thomas A. and Bruns, William: *Winning is Everything and Other American Myths*. New York, Macmillan, 1976.
41. Weiss, Paul: *Sport: A Philosophic Inquiry*. Carbondale, SIU U Pr, 1969.
42. Whitehead, Alfred N.: *Adventures of Ideas*. New York, Macmillan, 1933.

SUPPLEMENTARY READINGS

The following entries are related to the text presentation on the subject of ethics and ethical decisions in physical education and sport. The texts which deal directly with ethics and philosophy will support and strengthen the presentation of ethical theories. The texts which treat sport from a psychological and sociological view will serve to provide a more comprehensive context within which the ethics of physical education and sport reside.

Alderman, Richard B.: *Psychological Behavior in Sport.* Philadelphia, Saunders, 1974.

Bahm, Archie: *Ethics As a Behavioral Science.* Springfield, Thomas, 1974.

Baier, Kurt: *The Moral Point of View: A Rational Basis of Ethics.* Ithaca, Cornell U Pr, 1960.

Bourke, Vernon J.: *Ethics: A Textbook in Moral Philosophy.* New York, Macmillan, 1958.

Bradley, Francis H.: *Ethical Studies.* New York, Liberal Arts Pr., 1951.

Brandt, Richard B.: *Ethical Theory: The Problems of Normative and Critical Ethics.* Englewood Cliffs, N.J., P-H, 1959.

Brennan, Joseph Gerard: *Ethics and Morals.* New York, Har-Row, 1973.

Burr, John R. and Goldwiger, Mitton: *Philosophy and Contemporary Issues.* New York, Macmillan, 1972.

Carr-Saunders, A. M. and Wilson, P. W.: *The Professions.* London, Frank Cass and Co. Ltd., 1964.

Cratty, Bryant J.: *Children and Youth in Competitive Sports.* Mt. Prospect, Ill., Ed Direct, 1974.

Dewey, John: *Human Nature and Conduct.* New York, HR&W, reprinted in Westminister, Md., Random, 1922.

———— : *Theory of the Moral Life.* New York, HR&W, 1960.

Dickey, Glenn: *The Jock Empire; Its Rise and Deserved Fall.* Radnor, Penn., Chilton, 1974.

Edwards, Harry: *Sociology of Sport.* Homewood, Ill., Dorsey, 1973.

Frankena, William K.: *Ethics.* Englewood Cliffs, N.J., P-H, 1963.

Gardner, Paul: *Nice Guys Finish Last; Sport and American Life.* New York, Universe, 1975.

Green, Thomas H.: *Prolegomena to Ethics.* 5th ed. Oxford, Clarendon, 1929.

Johannesen, Richard L.: *Ethics in Human Communication.* Columbus, Ohio, Merrill, 1975.

Kattsoff, Louis O.: *Making Moral Decisions: An Existential Analysis.* The Hague, Netherlands, Martinus Nijhoff, 1965.

Kimpel, Ben: *Principles of Moral Philosophy.* New York, Philes Lib, 1960.

Kurtz, Paul: *Decision and the Condition of Man.* Seattle, U of Wash Pr, 1965.

Ladd, John (Ed.): *Ethical Relativism.* Belmont, Calif., Wadsworth Pub, 1973.

Michener, James R.: *Sports in America.* New York, Random, 1976.

Miller, Donna Mae: *Coaching the Female Athlete.* Philadelphia, Lea & Febiger, 1974.

Murray, Gilbert: *Stoic, Christian and Humanist.* London, Watts, 1940.

Niebuhr, Reinhold: *An Interpretation of Christian Ethics.* New York, Meridian, 1956.

Nixon, Howard L.: *Sports and Social Organization.* Indianapolis, Bobbs, 1976.

Noll, Roger G. (Ed.): *Government and the Sports Business.* Washington, D.C., Brookings, 1974.

Novak, Michael: *The Joy of Sports; End Zones, Bases, Baskets, Balls, and the Consecration of the American Spirit.* New York, Basic, 1976.

Ogilvie, Bruce C. and Tutko, Thomas A.: *Problem Athletes and How to Handle Them.* London, Pelham, 1966.

Orlick, Terry and Botterill, Col: *Every Kid Can Win.* Chicago, Nelson-Hall, 1975.

Ralbovsky, Martin: *Lords of the Locker Room: The American Way of Coaching and Its Effect on Youth.* New York, Wyden, 1974.

Ross, Stephen D.: *Moral Decision: An Introduction to Ethics:* San Francisco, Freeman C, 1972.

Rushall, Brent S. and Siedentop, Darlyl: *The Development and Control and Behavior in Sport and Physical Education.* Philadelphia, Lea & Febiger, 1972.

Scott, Jack: *The Athletic Revolution.* New York, Free Pr, 1971.

Singer, Robert N.: *Coaching, Athletics and Psychology.* New York, McGraw, 1972.

———: *Myths and Truths in Sports Psychology.* New York, Har-Row, 1975.

Taylor, Paul W. (Ed.): *Problems of Moral Philosophy.* Belmont, Calif., Dickenson, 1967.

Tutko, Thomas A. and Tosi, Umberto: *Sports Psyching; Playing Your Best Game All of the Time.* New York, J P Tarcher, 1976.

VanderZwaag, Harold J.: *Toward a Philosophy of Sport.* Reading, Penn., A-W, 1972.

INDEX